Morris Academy
For Collaborative
Studies

I0448341

Our Path
to Social Justice

Foreword

The Class of 2024 at Morris Academy for Collaborative Studies has created the following work in collaboration with the Student Press Initiative at Columbia Teachers College. We are incredibly proud of the work students have created and are grateful for the opportunity to honor that work in this publication.

Our students are coming of age in a time of rapid social change that impacts them in direct and meaningful ways. Their writing explores topics of a wide range, discussing everything from climate change to criminal justice to the reform of our nation's healthcare system. Our research process broadened our students' understanding and knowledge of the topics they chose to explore, empowering them to craft nuanced claims about the social justice issues they have written about.

Our students' writing explores the intersections of their identities and reveals compelling arguments about topics they feel personally connected to. Our students, many of whom were born and raised in the Bronx, often live at the crossroads of compounding social inequities. As public consciousness grows and America's problems become more televised, our students' stories remind us these issues have always existed in the Bronx, New York.

As mass shootings become more normalized throughout the country, the alarming rate of gun violence in the Bronx continues to increase. While undocumented immigrants fight to legitimize their citizenship in a country that didn't welcome them, many of our students and their families remind us that immigrants are truly what makes America great. Each time our nation grapples with Earth's sustainability, this generation reminds us that climate change has always been a crisis for them. As police violence becomes more widely documented, they help us see that the criminal justice system is only fair to some. Our students remind us that the Bronx is beautiful, but their community deserves better.

This work heavily relies on credible research that reflects the reality of these social issues, and many students chose to incorporate their own personal narratives as anecdotal evidence of how these issues manifest in their worlds. This process broadened our students' understanding of the topics they felt most connected to, empowering them to become agents of change and encouraging us to leave this world a little bit better than we found it.

Sincerely,
Ms. Eryn Geller, Ms. Emily Bloodworth, and Ms. Stephanie Paz

Table of Contents

Majed Alsaidi

Chase Your Dreams

The Syrian Refugee Crisis has been one of the most challenging global issues of the 21st century. This crisis has had a really big consequences not only for the millions of Syrians who have been forced to flee their homes but for the entire international community.

This issue is so important because The current situation for Syrian refugees is extremely serious. There are now over 5.5 million Syrian refugees living in neighboring countries, and over 6 million internally displaced persons within Syria. These refugees are facing huge challenges, such as lack of access to proper medical care, education, shelter, food, and clean water. These individuals are often living in overcrowded refugee camps with limited access to basic needs, and many are at risk of exploitation and abuse.

The Syrian Refugee Crisis can be traced back to the political unrest that began in 2011. In March of that year, protests broke out in Syria, demanding democratic reforms and the resignation of President Bashar alAssad. These protests quickly turned into a "full fledged armed conflict when the government responded with violent repression, leading to the formation of various opposition groups" (SOURCE). This conflict is now in its seventh year, and the impact has been catastrophic for Syrians, with over 500,000 people killed and over 12 million displaced (SOURCE). the UN an many other countries around the world have taken measures to accept Syrian refugees. Some countries, such as Germany and Canada, have been particularly generous in their willingness to accept refugees (SOURCE). However, other countries have been less welcoming. Many have implemented strict border policies that have made it difficult for Syrian refugees to enter their countries, despite the urgent need for help (SOURCE).

In 2023 there are about An estimated 15.3 million syrian refugees that needed life saving support and 5.5 million refugee that applied for asylum in neighboring country like Egypt, turkey, Yemen, iraq and couple other in the USA, Canada, europe.

In conclusion, the Syrian refugee crisis is one of the most serious global issues of our time. It has had significant consequences for millions of Syrians and the international community and the conflicts in Syria is ongoing, and unless the root causes are addressed, it is unlikely that the crisis will be resolved. The internationel community must continue to provide aid and support to Syrian refugees, and more countries must be willing to accept them. Only through a donation and other countries helping can we hope to decrease the suffering of those affacted by this crisis.

Miranda Amill

Mental Illness

What is Mental Illness? Mental Illness are health conditions involving changes in the emotions, thoughts, and actions/ behaviors of someone. Mental health is a very important topic/social issue to make sure people are changing and being helped deal with their mental illness. Mental Illness impacts everyone, there is ot discrimination when it comes to mental illness. Mental illness is important because everyone deals with it, no matter where you come from or what you look like. People with mental illnesses get treated differently making it harder for these people dealing with mental illness to get better emotionally.

Mental illness impacts everyone, there is no discrimination when it comes to mental illness. Mental illness is important because everyone deals with it, no matter where you come from or what you look like. "8.4% of 21 million people deal with Depression" (National Alliance Of Mental Illness) People everywhere are dealing with this illness and it's hard to deal with. Depression doesn't just happen to adults, it happens to children and or teenagers. "Mental illnesses are common in the United States. It is estimated that more than one in five U.S. adults live with a mental illness (57.8 million in 2021)." This shows that a lot more people suffer with mental illness than others actually think.

Diagnoses of mental illnesses were being made as far back as the Ggreeks. In 1883 a German psychiatrist published a system of psychological disorders with a pattern of symptoms that underline the cause of psychological issues. (History of Mental Illness Hostos Community College). A real advocate for mental illness is Demi Lovato. Demi Lovato deals with bipolar disorder, addiction, and bulimia. She has had suicidal thoughts in the past. She has mental health issues of her own, which is why she cares about her and her fans' mental health. Her speaking out is to show that cCelebrities have mental health issues like anyone else in the world. It shows that people aren't alone and people deal with mental issues of their own. She wants to make sure people can talk to others about what is going on with their own mental state. Her speaking out will give people the hope and have others to speak out on their own as well.

A man with schizophrenia was being mistreated due to his mental illness. He was in jail for 3 weeks naked and malnourished. She was in solitary confinement. People who don't understand someone with a mental illness treat people with mental illnesses horribly. It creates more hurt in the person's mind and makes them feel not normal. Which can make their condition worse.

Mental Illness impacts everyone, there is no discrimination when it comes to mental illness. Mental illness is important because everyone deals with it, no matter where you come from or what you look like. I hope that people would understand others with mental illnesses better and not mistreat them. Try to get to know them because they need someone to be there for them.

Betsy Balbuena

To The People Listening

Every day we are getting closer to not being able to reverse the effects of climate change. We need to take initiative and action in order to help save our earth and maintain equilibrium. As regular people, we don't notice and realize how we are enduring the effects of climate change. Have you ever thought about why it's so cold in the middle of what's supposed to be spring? Or why sometimes it rarely snows in areas that typically experience severe blizzards? Well, it's all because of climate change.

When I was younger, I didn't realize climate change was a thing. I used to think of earth day - a day to protect and support the environment - as a day to spend drawing pictures of the Earth and coloring it in bright blue and green- and as we look at the Earth now, it isn't so light blue and green. It is important to educate youth and everyone around about climate change and help them make changes in their everyday lives in order to produce less greenhouse gas emissions and also help the environment become a healthier place.

As humans, We produce an abundance of emissions as a result of everything we do, but reducing these emissions doesn't have to be difficult. We can change the ways we travel, keep connected, stay cool and warm, and produce items. It's up to us to bring about change, and speaking up for what's right can have a positive impact. As long as our planet continues to meet all of our needs, we don't want to destroy it. Our carbon footprint, or the quantity of greenhouse gas emissions we produce as a result of our daily activities, must be taken into consideration in order to fully understand our influence. Small adjustments to our daily routines, such as unplugging unnecessary items, recycling, and using reusable containers, can have a significant impact.

Beyond simply altering our everyday habits, there are other actions we can do to address the urgent problem of climate change. For instance, pursuing a career in science, math, or engineering can aid in the creation of eco-friendly innovations and long-term fixes to the problems that cause climate change. We have the ability to change things as the following generation of scientists.

We need to stop and we need to stop now. There is going to be a point where changes can't be irreversible and where we as people won't be able to change the inevitable. One might not be able to make a difference, but together we can.

Thank you for your time.

Griznell Baltodano

Injustice

There are many social justice issues impacting the world today. One problem that people are trying to address is immigration. Immigration is undocumented people migrating to a different country. This situation impacts the citizens of that country and those migrating. People are fighting to help these people because it is illegal to migrate from one country to another with no documents. This issue is important because many people either die or are put into cages like if they were animals. Many immigrants are treated very unfairly and usually are looking for a better life. There are many protests and marches held to fight for those trying to become citizens and work towards their dream life.

It's important to care about immigration because it's a problem that affects people's lives and injustice. One data point that concerns this issue is Arizona S.B 1070 that was introduced around 2010, which is a law that has been enforced to encourage racial profiling for undocumented immigrants. This issue also gave authority to detain anyone.

This impacts immigrants because this law is more against them being able to live as a free human with their own rights. Another data point that concerns this issue is "brothers in texas arrested after 2 migrants shot, one fatally, near U.S. -mexico border" (www. cbsnews.com). This means that two white brothers that are from Texas, United States had the intention to shoot and kill these two migrants coming from another country. This impacts other immigrants because in some cases American citizens can be ignorant and not support immigrants migrating to the U.S. If this issue is not addressed, then immigrants will continue to face injustice and be treated unfairly.

One event that happened in this issue's history was Ellis Island. Ellis island is a small island located in New York City, which began receiving arriving immigrants on new years day, 1892. The structure that was placed in Ellis Island began by looking over the immigrants documents and if the person was in stable condition. The documents estimated the amount of time the inspection process would last for. Only 2% of arriving immigrants were excluded from entry. A diagnosed disease that is contagious that could endanger public health, would be one reason why they would be excluded from entry. The other reason that would lead you to being excluded is a legal inspector who was concerned an immigrant would likely become a public charge or an illegal contract laborer. This event was important because this is how immigrants first got to America and how the process was many years ago. Another event that happened in history was Bookings which took place from 1960 to 2019. The event began in the early 1900s when white people migrated from other countries illegally but faced no consequences including deportation or threat of apprehension. In contrast many people of color are facing these consequences, mainly latinos. Latinos are being stripped of their human rights and having no access to any privileges. This was often in the context of racialized debates targeted at latinos. One person who was fighting to change within this issue was Dolores Huerta. She believed in tackling head-on and was comfortable handling many confrontations.

One event that recently occurred in late september 2022 is "Brothers in texas arrested after 2 migrants shot, one fatally, near U.S. -Mexico border" reported by CBS News. About 90 miles from El Paso, Texas, in Hudspeth county the two victims were among a group of other migrants getting water. The group acknowledged the two brothers passing by in the truck but quickly took cover when they realized the truck started to back up. One victim fatally died and the woman is transported and recovering at a nearby hospital. This event is important because it comes into play that many immigrants are forced to face injustice with no reasoning. Another event that happened recently was the Muslim Travel Ban. This event happened in America which began in late January 2017. President Trump signed an executive order to ban the United States from traveling to 7 muslim countries (Iran, Iraq, Libya, Somalia, Sudan, Syria and Yemen) for around 90 days. The order sparked many protests across the country at airports and civil liberties organizations. This event was important because it's an example of religious discrimination. One law that was recently passed that impacts this issue is the Anti Terrorism border protection and immigration reform act. This law was introduced in 2005, to place systematic surveillance using unmanned aerial vehicles, ground based sensors, satellites, radar coverage and cameras on international land and marine borders to prevent "potential terrorist" coming to the United States. One person who is fighting to change within this issue was Erika Andiola. She believed in fighting for migrants rights and to protect immigrants.

In conclusion, Immigration is something we should all care about. It's important to care about immigration because it's an ongoing issue that needs to be addressed and changed. This issue is progressively getting more negative as the years go by and causes many other issues to form. In the future, I believe one day immigration would be changed for the better and justice would be served for those who were negatively affected by wanting the chance to have a better life but instead faced injustice.

Jimmy Barbecho

The Life of an Immigrant in NYC

Being an immigrant means living a life of fear - the fear of being discriminated against, arrested, separated from your family, and far more, but nothing compares to the fear of being deported. I know this personally because I am a child of immigrants and live in a community where there is a multitude of people just like my parents. One of the best things about living in New York City is being able to see similar communities throughout the 5 boroughs, but these types of communities aren't everywhere. I realized this when I would go to different parts of the city with my dad when he brought me to work with him .

My dad would tell me stories about when he first got to this country and how hard it was for immigrants to find work, along with other obstacles they had to face. Luckily, his older brother (my uncle) arrived in the U.S 2 years prior and his boss gave my dad a job in construction too. He would tell me that one of the hardest parts about working in the city was not knowing English. He took English classes in the night after work to try to improve but it still wouldn't be perfect. He would always try to speak English to the best of his ability because he's seen how cruel some people can be towards immigrants, especially construction workers. Working in the Upper East Side, a predominantly white neighborhood, he's seen firsthand how immigrants get looked down upon and he's always tried to avoid that experience. He's taught me to always stand up for other immigrant workers because he would have also been thankful if someone stood up for him when he was new to this country.

I've been going to work with my dad since I was about 8 years old (2014), and I enjoyed it because I would rarely see him at home (working long hours is common in an immigrant household if given the opportunity). Depending on the urgency of a job, my dad would sometimes work 10-14 hours a day. During these long hours, as a kid I was really bored. I knew nothing about construction besides the fact that it's the skill of fixing or building structures. He usually brought me along to hand him tools, go buy supplies while he continued working, or if he needed help painting wall edges.

During the summer when I was 10 years old, I went to work with my dad in the Upper East Side of Manhattan. I remember taking the 4 train to 86 st and Lexington Ave and then having to walk about 15 minutes with my small legs. Before arriving at the job site, we stopped at a 7/11 to get breakfast. As soon as we walked in, you could smell the sweet aroma of coffee, the dryness of the pizza, and the juiciness of the hotdogs. My dad got a coffee with a croissant, as usual, and I got a fruit punch Gatorade with a small bag of original Lays (I know it wasn't the healthiest option but it was my favorite). We got our breakfast and went to the job site. My uncle had arrived before us and he had started working already. My dad realized that he forgot to bring some items with him, so he sent me to a nearby hardware store to buy a hammer, a box of nails, and electrical tape. Even though I was so young, it wasn't the first time that my dad had sent me out to buy tools or supplies. He would usually send if he left certain tools/supplies at another job site or he ran out of something and needed them for a current job.

Manhattan is a huge city and I was always scared of getting lost, but I successfully made it to the hardware store. As I walked around the store, I noticed there were a couple of people already inside so I tried to hurry up to avoid waiting in a long line. When I got on line there were already 3 people in front of me so I patiently waited. I noticed that the guy behind the counter was screaming at a customer. I didn't know what was happening until it all came together. The guy being screamed at was an immigrant worker and the guy behind the counter was kicking him out. He told the worker "How can I help you if you don't speak English? Go back to your country! We don't want your kind here. AFUERA!"

After I bought my items, I ran outside so I could catch up to the worker and asked him what he needed. He showed me a list that he had made on the back of some receipts and gave me the money I needed to go buy his items. The situation could have been avoided easily. The guy behind the counter could have done multiple things to try to help the worker. For instance, he could have asked if there was anyone in the store that spoke Spanish to help translate. Or he could have used an online translator like Google Translate to help the customer. I helped the worker because I learned a very valuable lesson from my dad: to always help an immigrant in need.

Overall, this type of discrimination toward immigrants occurs all the time in this country, especially in Republican states where most people are against immigrants trying to get residency or citizenship. Even though many immigrants came into this country illegally, they are still a very important part of society, as they are what makes this country so great. They deserve to be treated equally and to be able to experience the same opportunities as U.S. citizens.

Crystalyn Boahene

Immigration

The concept of creating a fair, just and equitable society in which every individual has equal access to opportunities and rights, regardless of their race, gender, religion, sexual orientation or socioeconomic status is what I refer to as social justice. Social justice is the fair treatment and equitable status of all individuals and social groups within a state or society. Social justice issues of grave importance include: incarceration, gun violence, healthcare, police brutality,and racism. These are only a few examples of social justice that affect American society and the nation at wide today. While these issues are of critical importance to society, one social justice issue worth mentioning is immigration and its impact on American society over the past few hundred years.

Migration is the movement of people or animals from one place to another whereas immigration is the international movement of people to a destination country of which they are not natives or where they do not possess citizenship in order to settle as a permanent resident or naturalized citizen. In other words, it is the movement of people from one country to another permanently or temporarily. This is an issue of social justice because it involves questions of fairness, equity and human rights.

It has been a crucial aspect of human history with people from different countries and cultures continually migrating for thousands of years. As such, it is considered to be a global phenomenon that shapes the human experience and impacts society and the economy. People are striving to fight to help immigrants. People who know their rights, people who have empathy and know their rights. For the past years, people who have migrated have been treated illy. They are regarded with no respect. Why is that, you may ask? There are many factors. This issue is important because immigrants are forced to live in fear of deportation. People migrate for various reasons such as work, education, or to reunite with family members. Some sought a better life, some fled oppression, and some were moved against their will. The history of the United States has always been shaped by people and communities who came to its shores or moved within its borders. One data point that concerns the issue is it involves promoting fairness in the distribution of resources, opportunities and privileges as well as removing barriers that prevent people from fully participating in society.

One data point that concerns the issue is racial discrimination. PBS learning media said "A clear example of this was the Chinese Exclusion Act signed into law by President Chester in 1882 which prohibited Chinese laborers from migrating to the US. Chinese men faced severe discrimination, violence and job competition from white laborers. The policies separated families and had long-lasting impacts on Chinese American communities. It reinforced the idea that Chinese immigrants were inferior and undeserving of the same privileges as white Americans."

The American society over the years advanced and with such advancements came about positive policies and measures which helped to improve the livelihoods of immigrants. A clear example was the primary inspection station set up for immigrants on Ellis Island. Here, doctors would examine them for any contagious diseases while inspectors would review their paperwork and conduct interviews to ensure they were not criminals. Though lengthy, the process of passing through Ellis Island was a symbol of hope and opportunity, a chance to start a new life in a new country. Today, Ellis Island is home to the Ellis Island National Museum of Immigration which explains the history and experiences of these immigrants in greater detail.

Recently, there have been events and policies that have been passed. One event that happened recently was the family separation and detention. It happened in the United States in the year 2018. During this event, The department of homeland security referred all immigrants who moved to the US without authorization to the department of justice for prosecution. This event is important because the attorney generals initiated this program which was to stop the illegal migration process. One law that was recently passed that impacts the issue is Operation streamline. This policy stated that federal criminal charges are brought against individuals apprehended crossing the border illegally. This is important because the individuals who were affected were the migrants from different races whereby they were sent to prison or prosecuted. There was a lot of misallocation of resources ,criminalisation and financial cost increase. Finally, one person who is fighting to change within this issue was Norman Mineta. Norman Mineta was Japanese American who was sent to war ‖ internment camp in the 1990s. He was imprisoned by his own government and used that experience to inspire George W. Bush. On 11th september 2001, his leadership as a US secretary of transportation ensured that what happened to Japanese americans in the WW‖ would not happen again to any other group based on ethnicity or religion. One way this person advocated for change was after he got out of prison and tried to make things better by making sure that the Japanese experience which he had when he was a kid was the Japanese in San Jose who were accused of the pearl harbor incident.

Quite a lot has been done throughout the years but there's still more work to be done. I agree that there's a need to strengthen our borders. Let's always have it in mind, though we may be different in color, nationality, gender or race, there's always strength in unity. The socioeconomic development of America relies on the combined efforts of its natives and immigrants as well. Let's indeed make America the land of opportunity.

Works cited

Immigration: https://www.splcenter.org/issues/immigrant-justice   01 April 2020

"During this event,..."Migrants and refugees: https://news.un.org/en/news/topic/migrants-and-refugees 29th march 2023

"Norman Mineta was Japanese American ..."Family separation: American Bar Association March 27th 2023   https://www.americanbar.org/advocacy/governmental_legislative_work/priorities_policy/immigration/familyseparation/

"Ellis Island" https://www.history.com/topics/immigration/ellis-island#:~:text=Ellis%20Island%20is%20a%20historical,immigrants%20 pass%20 through%20its%20 doors

"Chinese Exclusion Act signed..." https://ny.pbslearningmedia.org/resource/the-chinese-exclusion-act/asian-americans-video/

Operation Streamline https://immigrationforum.org/article/fact-sheet-operation-streamline/

Mineta https://www.history.com/topics/immigration/asian-american-timeline published march 22,2021

Hector Bueno

Gun Violence

There are many social justice issues that I believe that have to be addressed, but the one that I believe that needs to be addressed most is gun violence. Gun violence is a topic that has been often debated for hundreds of years.Gun violence is a social justice issue that needs to be addressed because the rate of gun violence has gone up for more than 10 times of how it was during the year 2000 that also means the amount of suicides and people who are unintentionally shot has increase . Since the increase of gun violence the the amount of people that gun violence impacts has also increased and because of this a lot of more people die every year. Gun violence is a social justice issue that needs to be solved because it has been affecting too many people and it seems to be very easy for people to get access to guns.

Gun violence needs to be addressed because the number of people that is affecting has continued to increase and has not stopped. Gun violence is not just killing someone with a gun. Also suicides or homicide using guns is consider part of gun violence. Vital City found out that New York City has the largest homicide rate of 2019 and 2020 per 100,000 people, Brooklyn has the highest shooting incident from 2020 and 2021 and that "117,183 americans have die of gun suicides from 2015 to 2019". This shows how gun violence is affecting more and more people and it does not seem to be decreasing because people have too much access to guns.

Gun violence is a social justice issue that needs the most attention to be solved because people have the right to have guns and this is due to the second amendment. The second amendment is a law that gives Americans the right to bear arms so any American could have a gun because of the second amendment. One major event that impacted the issue of gun violence was in 1791 when the second amendment was passed. This event impacted this issue because the second amendment is the law that gives americans the right to bear arms. Another event that impacted this social justice issue was in 1963 When the 35th president of the United States John F. Kennedy was assassinated. This event impacted the issue of gun violence because JFK was the youngest President of the U.S to die because of gun violence(Longley) and this only happened because of the right that the second amendment gives any Americans. Although Many laws have been passed about gun violence those laws have not impacted gun violence very much and this is because of the second amendment that gives Americans the right to bear arms. In 1966 the Mulford law said the people could only carry loaded guns as long as they had a permit (PBS). That means that people if they want can alway carry a gun on them the only thing that they most have is a permit. Today gun violence is one of the biggest social justice issues because people have the ability to have and carry guns on them.

Another reason why gun violence is a social justice issue that needs the most attention to be solved is because of the accessibility that people have to guns. People have too much accessibility to guns because they have the right to bear arms but this also leads to the possibility of teens having guns as it shows from some recent events.. One recent event that has happened was the Uvalde school shooting. The Uvalde school shooting is an event that happened on May 24 2022 when a 18 year old high school student suddenly went into an elementary school and killed 19 children and two teachers (Holston). He also shot his grandmother before crashing a vehicle near the school (Holston). . This event was important because it drew the attention of the government because of how a 18 year old high school student was able to accuair a firearm and kill 19 children and 2 teachers from an elementary school. This event influences gun violence because it shows how easy it is for Americans to get a gun because of the second amendment. Also another event that happened was the Parkland school shooting on Feb 14 2018. This is an important event because this happened when 19 year old Nikolas Cruz went into his former high school in Parkland Florida and started shooting people with a semi-automatic rifle killing 17 people and wounded 14 more people (Chuck, Johnson, and Siemaszko). This changed a lot about gun violence because it helped to pass 50 more gun control laws after a movement led by the student survivors of that mass shooting in Parkland.

In conclusion, gun violence is a social justice issue that we should all care about. We should care about gun violence because gun violence is affecting a lot more people than what it used to. This is important because more and more people are dying because of gun violence and also people have too much accessibility to gun violence. In the future there could be less gun violence but that is if people help to create new laws that help remove guns from the streets and people that should not have then also they need to make it a lot harder for people to get guns, as it shows that even people that are in their teens have the ability to get a gun.

Work cited

Chuck Elizabeth, Johnson Alex and Siemaszko Corky "17 killed in mass shooting at high school in Parkland, Florida"

https://www.nbcnews.com/news/us-news/police-respond-shooting-parkland-florida-high-school-n848101

23 March 2023

Holston Kenny "A Partial List of Mass Shootings in the United States in 2022"

https://www.nytimes.com/article/mass-shootings-2022.html

23 March 2023

Vital City "Making relevant data accessible to the public to help better understand and improve public safety"

https://www.vitalcitynyc.org/data_hub?tag=Gun+violence

10 March 2023

ABC News "By the Numbers: America has a gun violence problem"

https://www.youtube.com/watch?v=JezDvhYM-4I

10 March 2023

Longley Robert "Timeline of Gun Control in the United States"

https://www.thoughtco.com/us-gun-control-timeline-3963620

14 March 2023

PBS "State capitol March

https://www.pbs.org/hueypnewton/actions/actions_capitolmarch.html

14 March 2023

Giancarlos Carillo

Gun Violence

There are many social justice issues impacting the world today. One problem that people are trying to address is Gun Violence. Gun Violence is a very big issue in our community and it impacts people that are colored. People are fighting to help decrease gun violence. This issue is important because people are scared to attend school.

It's important to care about Gun Violence because there is nothing being done to decrease Gun Violence. One data point that concerns this issue was 647 mass shootings in 2022. This means that there is no background check for guns. This impacts the safety of the public. Another data point that concerns this issue is Firearms are involved in 79% of all homicides. This means that firearms are mostly used to kill one person. This impacts the African American Community. If this issue is not addressed, more people can get their hands on guns from unlicensed gun dealers.

One event that happened in this issue's history was The Assasination of John F Kennedy. It happened in Dallas, Texas in 1963. During the event John F Kennedy was assassinated while riding in a presidential motorcade through Dealey Plaza. This event was important because his assassination became history.

Another event that happened in history was The Assassination of Martin Luther King Jr. it happened at The Lorraine Motel in 1968. During This event Martin Luther King Jr and his associates were staying at The Lorraine Motel on the second floor balcony when he was struck in the neck with a sniper bullet. This event was important because Martin Luther King was known for leading the civil rights movement to end segregation. One law that was passed in the past was The Gun Control Act of 1968. This law said that it prohibits guns to certain people and runs background checks on gun dealers. It was important because the act banned guns on drug addicts and mentally ill people. Finally, one person who was fighting to change within this issue was Lyndon B. Johnson. They wanted to include a minimum age requirement to purchase a firearm.

One event that happened recently was The Uvalde Texas School Shooting. It happened at Robb Elementary School in 2022. During this event 19 students and 2 teachers were killed by a gunman. This event is important because the Robb Elementary School Shooting was the worst school shooting in texas. Another event that happened recently was The Marjory Stoneman Douglas high school shooting. It happened in Parkland, Florida in 2018. During this event 17 students were murdered and 17 were injured. This event was important because weeks after the school shooting people were protesting to end gun violence. One law that was recently passed that impacts this issue is The USA Background Check. This law says that it is required to run information through an FBI Database before a sale is made. It is important because it helps people from buying guns with a criminal record. Finally, one person who is fighting to change within this issue was Sybrina Fulton. They wanted to make a difference in the world by bringing awareness to senseless Gun Violence.

In Conclusion Gun Violence is something we should all care about. It's important to care about Gun Violence because it is a big issue that affects The Community. In the future There will be heavy strict rules on Gun Control and Heavier Security.

Gun Violence

My social justice is gun violence. Everyone is impacted by it because too many people are dying from it. People are fighting for gun safety because of all the deaths that have been happening in the past few years. My social issue is very important because not only are people dying because of it but people don't feel safe to walk down the street.

It's important to care about gun violence because there's so many people dying from it and being injured. One data point that concerns this issue is more than 500 people die every day because of violence committed with firearms. This means that gun violence is getting really bad through the years. The impact is that we are losing a lot of people to gun violence. Another data point that concerns this issue is 48,830 people died from gun-related injuries in the U.S., according to the CDC. This means that the number is going to keep increasing. This issue is affecting a lot of people and their families. If this issue is not addressed, then we are going to keep losing so many people.

One event that impacted the issue of gun violence was on November 22,1963, When Lee Harvey Oswald shot John F Kennedy in the dealer plaza in downtown Dallas,Texas. During this event Lee Havery Oswald was fighting for something different than John F Kennedy. This event was important by traumatizing a nation and led a united Congress to make a constitutional change. Another event that impacted the issue was in April 4,1968, when James Earl shot Martin Luther King while he was standing on his balcony outside his second floor room at Lorraine motel in Memphis,Tennessee. James Earl shot Martin Luther King because James was an outspoken racist. Today, More than 30 states allow the open carrying of a handgun without any license or permit, although in some cases the gun must be unloaded. One law that was passed in the past was ratified in 1789, The U.S constitution was passed by James Madison. The second amendment is "A well regulated militia, being necessary to the security of a free state, the right of people to keep and bear arms shall not be infringed". Which means people can carry guns.

One event that recently happened was on February 14,2018 in Parkland,Florida. During this event Nikolas Cruz was an expelled student because of a fight. He entered Marjory stoneman Douglas highschool and opened fire killing 17 and wounding 17 others. He decided to open fire because he was treated badly during attending the school and he bought the gun legally due to not having any ban. Another event that recently happened was On May 24, 2022, a gunman, armed with multiple weapons and wearing body armor, entered Robb Elementary School in Uvalde, Texas and killed 19 children and two teachers. He also shot his grandmother before crashing a vehicle near the school. Another example of an event or policy that influences gun violence is the assault weapon ban in 1994. This law banned the sale, transfer ,manufacturing and importation of semiautomatic weapons. This ban expired in 2003. Assault weapons and high-capacity magazines are frequently used in the violence that plagues our nation. Of all mass shooting incidents between 2009 and 2018, assault weapons accounted for 25% of deaths and 76% of nonfatal injuries. An advocate is Joe Biden is a gun violence activist. This person cares so much about this social justice issue because the gun violence increased after the ban expired. They were personally affected because all the people were losing due to gun violence.This experience inspired them to take action, by making his push for an assault weapons ban during his State of the Union address on Tuesday.

Gun violence is getting worse by the years if we don't implement a law for it to get worse. It's important because we need to come together and fix this issue. I hope that I'm a few years there's a law that can stop all the gun violence for good.

David Cervantes

Global Warming

One day, in middle school, our teacher put on a video about global warming that would show what would happen if we continue polluting the earth. Unfortunately, my teacher would not go into further detail about what would happen and just gave us a brief overview about how the world is getting warmer and this would lead to disastrous effects. My teacher not giving a good explanation of the global warming timeline, would lead many of my friends to believe that the world would be ending within the coming years. The next day, our teacher would have us do an activity asking us to find ways to slow down global warming. Many of my classmates would say things such as recycling and clean energy sources. After this, my friends and I would discuss what we would do to try to stop global warming if we had the money to. We would come up with joke answers such as sending all the garbage into space or destroying all the factories. We would joke around and act as if we didn't care as we believed that we had all the time in the world due to the fact that we were kids. While at the time we were joking, I knew that we were all thinking about how this would affect us later on in life and whether or not we would even make it to college.

Suddenly I realized if global warming continues, there won't be a world for me to grow up in. This led me to find ways to try to do my part in slowing global warming. I would try doing things such as recycling and organizing my garbage into the correct bins. Since at the time we didn't own a car or anything that used up a lot of energy, I wasn't concerned about my carbon footprint or my energy usage. While I would try my best to do my part in stopping global warming, I would eventually lose interest since I didn't have time to do any more research. I would essentially forget about the issue as I had stopped researching it. This wouldn't be just me though, most people would just forget about it, and those who were still worried about it would just be laughed at. (Side Note: This is all before the term was officially changed to climate change)

It wouldn't be until 10th grade, that I would have to do a project that talks about climate change and how it affects each coast of the US. I would gain a new understanding that the world isn't just getting hotter, but instead climate around it making drastic changes. These changes are more disastrous storms such as hurricanes and tornadoes. These are becoming more frequent as well as becoming more powerful as time passes. However, storms aren't the only things that are changing, the ocean would also change drastically. Both sea level and sea temperatures would begin to rise, completely changing ecosystems. On the other hand, droughts and wildfires would become more common due to the fact that some areas would go without rain or be extremely dry from the change in weather patterns caused by climate change. This would bring up the issue again but rather than panic, I would just think about how there isn't much for me to do to slow down global warming, I would just have to wait and see the results of what these large companies would do to try to appear that they care what happens with global warming. Of course, I would lose interest in the topic again and completely forget about the issue until it was brought up again.

Chinwendu Chibuzo

Immigration

There are many social justice issues impacting the world today. One problem that people are trying to address is immigration. Immigration is when someone moves out from their country to live in a foreign country permanently. IAnd it impacts foreigners because people tend to treat them differently. People are fighting to help immigration by fighting for the rights of immigrants in a foreign country. This issue is important because so many people support immigration and are ready to help those immigrants that are being discriminated against.

It's important to care about immigration because it's not fair to kick somebody out of the country just because they weren't born there. I don't think people who migrated from another country should be kicked out of the country just because they don't have rights. One data point that concerns this issue is poverty. This means that people who migrated from another country will not have a lot of money to help them out in the country. Most immigrants migrated to work or economic opportunities, to join family, or to study. Others move to escape conflict, persecution, terrorism, human rights violations, or employment opportunitiesy. This impacts immigrants to have a better opportunity in the country they migrated to. Another data point that concerns this issue is employment. This means that immigrants have a hard time being employed in a job that they are interested in. There are some common challenges for immigrants like forcing workers to labor long hours without paying overtime, not offering job training or protective equipment for dangerous jobs, and failing to let workers know of their legal rights. This impacts immigrants who are being treated differently at their jobs. If the issue is not addressed, then the issue would not change and people would keep treating immigrants differently.

One event that happened in this issue's history was Ellis Island. It happened in Ellis Island during 1855 to 1890. During this event, mMost immigrants went through the New York immigration station from 1855 to 1890. And most immigrants went through Ellis Island, which was mostly the only way. This event was important because Ellis Island was a transportation that most immigrants arrived in during this time period. Without the transportation of Ellis Island those immigrants probably wouldn't have migrated. Another event that happened in history was Latin American immigrants. During this event Latin American immigrants settled in America and started their lives in America. And during 1492 Christopher saw some tribes and demanded their money and gold. This event was important because it allowed Latin Americans people who migrated to live in America freely.

One law that was passed in the past was U.S visas. This law said that all immigrants need a U.S visa to travel abroad. It was important because it allows citizens of a foreign country who want to enter the United States generally to first get a U.S. visa, which is placed in the traveler's passport, a travel document issued by the traveler's country of citizenship. Finally, one person who was fighting to change within this issue was Jackie Chan. Jackie Chan was a young actor who was born in a poor village in Hong Kong. Jackie Chan's parents immigrated to Canberra, Australia. He impacted the issue of immigrants by showing the people that he can do anything in the acting industry. In the spring of 1822, the Chinese had an act called the "Chinese exclusion act immigration". It was a law that restricted Chinese people in the United States. This means that if Jackie Chan was born during this time period he would not be able to enter the United States and become an actor.

One event that happened recently in this issue's history was Muslim Travel Ban. It happened on January 27, 2017. During this event, Trump signed an executive order that banned people from traveling. Mainly Muslim countries like Iran, Iraq, Libya, Somalia, Sudan, Syria, and Yemen–and suspended the resettlement of all Syrian refugees. This event was important because this made a lot of muslims people stranded in their country and couldn't even travel. Also in 2020 the Trump administration expanded visa restrictions to six more countries - Eritrea, Kyrgyzstan, Myanmar, Nigeria, Sudan, and Tanzania. Another event that happened recently in history was The Wall. It happened in the U.S and Mexico during August 2017. During this event there was a barrier between the U.S. and Mexico. It separated many people from their family members for years. Some were deported to Mexico after having lived in the United States for decades without authorization. Some people never left Mexico, but have made their way to the fence to see relatives in the United States. This event was important because people need to understand what the Mexicans went through to stay away from their family. They were separated from their family and couldn't see them for a long time.

One law that was recently passed that impacts this issue is the American Dream and Promise Act. This law allowed undocumented immigrants in the United States to live freely with their communities. The Obama administration created the action for Childhood Arrivals program to help those who are called Dreamers. It is important because immigrants were able to live freely without having to worry about being discriminated against. Finally, one person who is fighting to change within this issue was Erika Andiolia. She wanted every immigrant to have their own rights in the community. She saw that a lot of immigrants were being treated differently so she made a change by protesting for the rights of all immigrants.

In conclusion Immigration is something we should all care about. It's important to care about Immigration because immigrants need to experience a new way of life. People who migrated to another country needed to be treated the same as the people in the country. In the future I want all immigrants to live happily in the area that they live in. I also want all immigrants to get all the rights that they deserve.

Jhon DeLaCruz

Gun Violence

When I was around 13 years old, I heard a strange noise outside. It sounded like a firework, so my immediate thought was that people were setting off fireworks outside so I went and looked out my window. All I saw was people screaming and running immediately after that all I saw were the police and the ambulance arriving.

As I continued looking outside, I found out that 2 people were shot. One of the people that got shot was extremely injured and the other dead right on the crime scene. This all happened in the Bronx. When I was looking outside I saw the bodies of the people that were shot. The first thing that I was thinking was What is happening? Why were there so many people? After that, I saw them put inside the ambulance. Whether it was because they had a grudge or some type of drug deal and owed money, whatever the cause was, the reasons for this shooting are still unknown to me.

Even though I didn't know the cause, I realized then that gun violence was a dangerous and serious issue. I learned more about shootings in the Bronx from the news. I kept seeing this same issue over and over again, but I never understood why. One day in 7th or 8th grade, I learned about gun violence in an American history class. I was interested in this topic because I kept seeing this over and over again. I then found out that gun violence is everywhere, even in history people had wars where countless people have died.

Gun violence is now the #1 leading cause of death for teenagers in the United States.. I am writing this to show people how dangerous the United States is and how many deaths have taken place due to this issue. If someone goes outside and is careful around their surroundings then maybe it could prevent many deaths. We can vote for people who support stricter gun laws and make sure that people's lives are no longer in danger.

Elizabeth Fernandez Gomez

Becoming In America

I was 9 years old when I first immigrated to the United States from the Dominican Republic. Of course, to the Bronx, NY, where Dominicans could be found everywhere up and down the fordham hill. Immigrating for better opportunities, education, legacy, future jobs and more that my 2 older brothers and I wouldn't have otherwise in La Vega, Dominican Republic. I was happy to see my mother after being separated for years where she'd go back and forth to the DR and the US. But how could I ever leave my family in DR alone. My grandparents who had helped raise me as my father worked everyday in his mechanic shop. Where my older cousin would take care of me, take me places and would call me her own daughter knowing my own mom was away living another life. In the state I'd have my mom though. The one person that stayed in my head when I rode under a tunnel back in DR. The one that I prayed to god every sunday as I was on my knees, hoping she'd come back for me.

I remember vividly seeing so many people in the JFK airport, all of whom would speak an entirely different language than what I grew up speaking. It wasn't until I got to the 4th grade that September of 2015, that I realized I had a long life task to do. Where I had to get accustomed to watching television in English and trying to pick up the "basics' '. Where I'd take Duolingo lessons on my mom's phone a few times a week and learned that "beber agua" is to drink water. I'd definitely learned the basics, my pronunciation was just really off. I lived in a small apartment in the Bronx, near Fordham and little Italy, with 2 bedrooms, and a small kitchen and bathroom and decent living room area.. In one room, my 2 brothers, my cousin and I would sleep in a bunk bed. The other, my aunt, mom and grandmother would sleep all in a queen sized bed. Money seemed to be short so I even understood that this was the most comfortable it was going to get for a while. My grandmother seemed bothered when she'd catch me watching Sofia the First in Spanish. "Tu no puede ver cosas en español hasta que sepas el inglés, después puedes ver lo que tu quieras"

That I couldn't watch things in Spanish until I knew english. I didn't want to learn English. I'd seen people speaking Spanish here and there, why couldn't I just find Spanish speaking people in school? Now what she said makes more sense. If I'm to live in the United States one of the things that will help me is to be fluent in English. I understand now that she was simply trying to help adjust with a place that simply wouldn't tolerate me speaking only spanish. Back then, I knew how to say I needed to use the bathroom, excuse me, thank you, my name is… all in a harsh accent which you could barely understand but it was there. 4th grade was hard. My first ever friend in the states was a short Mexican girl named Stephanie. She had long black hair and big eyes, I was so grateful that she spoke Spanish and could finally understand me. I'd try to speak English, but mostly I'd listen to her and ask for clarifications on how to say and pronounce words and sentences. During English class , I was put in the back of the classroom with other students who only knew Spanish to do computer lessons and games in English. It felt so surreal to feel like such an outcast. There was specifically this one girl, Angelina. Dirty Blond hair, a yellow sweater she'd always wear and a spiky personality. She was always jealous of me because I had apparently taken her best friend, Stephanie, away from her. She'd talk bad about me at the same table in english, knowing I wouldn't be able to understand, telling her friends how she could say anything and I wouldn't get it. It was true, but it hurt to find out from another bilingual girl at the table.

Going to the United States seemed like entering a different realm. The MTA buses were huge at first, it was so bizarre that you could pay with an orange card. The schools were enormous compared to the small one floor elementary school I used to attend in the Dominican Republic. The huge buildings seemed unreal to think about the building process. Growing up I began to realize that my education was crucial if I wanted something good in life. I didn't know then I had a very different education than those in other richer, whiter areas of New York. I would go to Manhattan once in a while and I was so surprised to only see White and East Asians there. My cousin who goes to a high school in Manhattan used to tell me how he was one of some other 4 kids there who looked like him, curly hair and tanned skin.

"Mi escuela esta llena de gringos y chinitos". He used to tell me.

I was lucky enough to look white myself. I knew that no one would 100% believe me if I were to tell them I was born and raised in the Dominican Republic. My mom on the other hand was definitely a brown woman. Short and short-tempered, who's simply the type to speak loud when talking normally, laughing without a care in the world like we were back in our rancho in the Dominican Republic. The type of person to call some-one out immediately if they are doing their job wrong. I still see her as this fearless and free person. She used to take the bus for an hour to a place where many latinos adults and parents would learn english and sometimes she'd take me. I wonder why she stopped going. She always seemed prepared but I guess not having the time really downed on her liberty to try and learn another language as a fully developed adult. Time she barely had, times where I wouldn't see her. On some days, she'd stay overnight with the elderly women she used to do home attend. I wouldn't see my mom for two whole days at a time because she simply needed the money for us. I remember begging for her to take me and we could sleep together, but she explained time and time again that the bed she had to sleep in was already so small and thin for her to be comfortable, there was no way we could sleep together. I worried constantly on those nights and I'd yearn to see her.

During the times when I was 13 to 14, I remember our family needing money badly. My 2 brothers and mothers along with my cousin had all been living in a one room apartment. Since my mom knew that wouldn't work for the five of us, she decided to split the room into two separate parts and cut the living room in half where another room would be installed. Sure it wasn't a lot of space since everything had been cut in half, but we were happy. We would talk every single day like a family and meet up in the small kitchen to cook together. Money was something that quickly limited our supplies though. One thanksgiving, my mom had absolutely nothing to buy food with, not even some savings. She had been worried the whole day wondering if she was going to be able to celebrate that day with us along with some food. Thankfully, that same evening she got paid and we were able to eat. None of us knew at the time she had struggled so much with money that even food was a question. We came to a place where we had to work and work and work. My oldest brother had to get a job when he was 17 and 18, leaving him with a massive amount of pressure to put money on the table and to be able to graduate. He himself had to sacrifice his education after high school and got our family in thou-sands of dollars in debt. It's important to recognize that no matter how much my family worked, they would still get 15 dollars an hour and it simply wasn't enough money to get rid of all the stress. With 4 children to take care of, my mom always tried her best to put food on the table but it still wasn't enough to the point where she could take a vacation. Many immigrants come to the states having no diploma or further education after high school, that in itself limits them in the labor department even if they have a lot of skill in a field. Education is key in the US and those who don't have "proper" education will always be looked down upon. Regardless, the way that society has constructed this idea of professionalism has to change because Black and Brown immigrants are the reason why the United States is one of the most successful countries, in many aspects. Besides bringing diversity and a loadsome of culture, Immigrants have built the states into more cities and still they have some of the most unfair disadvantages. My mom was automatically set up for failure because she didn't have the education required to succeed and be able to support her family, this is the same with many other immigrants who have to build themselves up from the very bottom and don't have the same opportunities as others who are native to a good place that cares about their education.

While much of this was going on, during the late months of 2020 and early 2021 I was specifically struggling with my mental health. Online school was really taking a toll on me and not just that. I had grown up in a household where school can be your ticket towards attention and admiration or it could be one's careless chore but it meant you wouldn't be seen academically. For me, I had to get good grades, I had to do all of my assignments and complete them to the best of my ability because what else did I have besides being a good student? Sure I had a couple common hobbies but none of them defined me like being an A+ student. The feeling of being bragged about to other parents, to be used as an example, to be told good job or I'm so proud of you are the words I would yearn for when giving my mom my report card. I would wake up everyday for online school at 8:55am, while having slept 6 hours, I'd manage to make it until class was over. I remember every single day being the same cycle of trying and trying. It felt endless and exhausting because I couldn't bring myself to do any more work when I had absolutely nothing to look forward to in the future. The idea that I could somehow bring wealth into the family slowly disappeared. My motivation for school and life was robbed every single day that I would take 2-3 hour naps and go to sleep at 3am to repeat everything again and I didn't care. But the thing is I did care. The back of my head was constantly yelling at me everyday that I needed to do work, that I couldn't just stop what I needed to do for a better future. I tried to do work but somehow social media and talking to my online friends was the only thing glued to my eyes. I would glance at my school laptop reading what needed to be done, and I wrote one thing and then I was back to doing not school work. I would procrastinate for hours and hours doing the same meaningless things over and over again. Most of all, I hated myself and the fact that I had always seemed to be

forgotten, that there was nothing to me as a person and I hated being such a boring person. I didn't mind how I looked, but I knew I wasn't such a nice person as I put myself to be. I don't know what drove me to believe I was so bad, but in my mind, I didn't deserve to live at all if I was simply just going to exist in a world I was exhausted of. There was a point where I felt I didn't really feel much anymore, mentally, but physically I supposed I always could. Social media teaches you ways into doing things and so what would be better than trying out ways into which I could cope with this depression. And so I started to self harm, starting out with a sharp nail from our toolbox. All it would do is scratch, it'll sting a bit but didn't really do much. To feel something I needed something that would cut so razors were the next best thing. It was crazy to think about how easily it could cut skin and draw out blood. Do a couple more swatches and I was done for the day. I don't know exactly why I did this. I didn't post on social media or talk to anyone besides my online friends in far away states. But somehow it helped me to think that maybe I deserved it. Because I wasn't doing what I was supposed to be doing. Soon enough I was talking to my doctor for an annual physical about mental health and I accidently mentioned something I shouldn't have back then. I said something about always feeling down and whatnot and feeling hopeless enough to do something I shouldn't be thinking about. A few minutes passed by and me and my mom were directed to the emergency room. I remember my mom being irritated the whole time she was there, telling me that I can't just say anything I want because they'll take it seriously and actually do something about it. I'm sorry mom, I didn't think they'd actually get me some help, I didn't know I just wanted to try. What she didn't know was that I was genuinely feeling unsafe. I couldn't go home because I was scared I was going to do something to myself, that I wasn't safe by myself because all the feelings of despair I felt would intensify. In the emergency room, I was panicking. My mom had gone out to get me something to eat and all I could do was think about what would happen next and the fact that I left my forensics zoom meeting. I could feel my own heart beating in the chaotic room, filled with other teens in their grippy socks and hospital gowns. Soon after, this woman in her 20s took me to a private area to talk. She asked me questions about attempting.
"If you were to kill yourself, how would you do it?'

I was shocked at her tone of questioning but I still just said I don't know. It was like she took this as just another suicidal teen, bored out of her hearing the same type of stories. She continued on with her questions in the same sort of tone. I was always caught off guard and left uncomfortably. This was when I realized that they were going to keep me in that emergency room. From March 8th till March 10th I stayed in that room and left that night to a psychiatric ward in Long Island. Once I got there, my mom cried as she came to realize that I was going to stay there alone for the night. Not just that night, but for two weeks I would be staying there alone.

That night I remember being completely lost in a place where other teens like me were. I had a roommate the first night who told me her story and why she was there. She said she didn't like people touching her hair because it reminded her of how her cousin would touch her whenever hed rape her. After that night she went home and I stayed in that room alone. I had realized that It was generally sad that someone from my background was at a psychiatric ward. A dominican daughter who always seemed so interested and intelligent in school, was now having conversations about what antidepressants would work best for her. I genuinely felt ashamed that I was in that position and questioned if my family back in DR knew enough about the situation and whether they were judging me for not being strong enough. I made some friends at the clinic and finally got out in late march. I still felt the need to still hide things. I couldn't express my feelings to my therapist and psychiatrist. I kept telling everyone that everything was fine now and that I felt better. But in reality, It didn't feel like I had a life changing outlook on life and the only motivation I had was to find something more meaningful.

That summer I went to the Dominican Republic for the first time in about 5 years. I had missed being in a place I had once called home, with the people that raised me and grew up by. The air felt lighter, like there wasn't such a constant reminder that I had to do something more and that I couldn't enjoy the things that made life better.

The financial problems were still there when I came back and stress didn't seem like it was leaving anytime soon. We had moved to a new apartment a little farther from fordham. Finally, I had my own spacious room and I was so excited to decorate it however I wanted it to. Things started looking up until we realized that rent was going to be $2,600 a month. Even with my mom and stepdad working, there was no way we could ever save up so much money and be able to pay off the thousands of dollars in debt. My older brother who had to drop out of college to work was also under an immense amount of stress. He was so smart in school and was looking forward to learning more about technology and computer science. It hurt so much to watch as slowly his dreams had to disappear because of money we didn't have. To watch as his education was timed as it was soon time to work long hours while barely getting paid to get rid of any debt and trying to pay bills. We can no longer live in a society where working families are getting paid the same, and the cost of living is only getting more expensive. If rent is going to increase everywhere then the wage should increase as well. This is a way in which black and brown children won't have to be so afraid of growing up and deteriorating their mental health for a better life. A way that immigrant daughters and sons can actually move up in the American dream they always envisioned and where their parents can finally think about retiring.

The Journey To
The Land of Freedom

As a young kid in middle school, I never knew how my parents immigrated to the U.S. until they sat me down to tell me about the story. In their young teenage years, my mom and dad fell in love during high school. My dad was a bit popular so it caused problems with their relationship, and it eventually came to an end. My dad wasn't really accepted by my mother's parents, so it was difficult to get their approval. He was seen as a person who would get into a lot of trouble so he was held back many times in school.

After finishing high school, my mom got pregnant with my older sister. Her grandparents were so furious that they would beat her and kick her out of the house. My uncles from my home side were already looking for a better life so they wanted to go to the U.S which the idea was passed on to my parents. My uncles were working from a young age helping out to have enough money to pay for bills and still go to school. The relationship between my grandparents and my uncles wasn't the best because they were abusive any time if they did something wrong or disobeyed them. They didn't want to experience this all the time, so they had to make a major decision for themselves.

They would always say that the U.S is the "land of freedom". The thing was they didn't have money to travel all the way to the U.S., so the only way was crossing the border. My parents left without telling her parents and leaving everything in the past wanting to give her kids a better life in the future. My uncles and parents paid a coyote to help them cross the border and get them as far as they can. My parents took a car to travel more and walk less so they are able to get there faster.

As they got closer to the security, they were stopped. Many things went through my mom head of whether or not they would get caught and put an end in their way to America. They were asking many questions to the driver, but it took a while for them to search the car. Anxious and scared, my parents tried their best not to make noise and to not panic. They searched and searched the car to find something wrong but nothing. They found nothing.

My parents were hiding under the car seat which was painful because of the baby that would be born soon. After getting to a certain point, they were left off in the middle of the desert. Having barely any food or water, they had to walk miles and miles. The only food that was around was nopales, and using its juices as a water supply was the only way to survive. Nothing else was in the desert except sand so what else would they be able to survive off. The night was freezing and the sun was blazing at them.

After some days, they came across border patrol hiding and ducking by using the hills as cover but a single turn of the border patrol caught a glimpse of them. Running and running as fast as they could to get away from them, my father was able to get away with ease but my mother was a different story. Being weak from the legs and being pregnant weighed her down caused her to get caught.

My father went on to the United States without my mother and made it to Phoenix, Arizona. He would go meet up with my uncle and drive up to New York to find a better place to live. During this time, my mom was sent to an immigration detention center where they put her fingerprints onto the system and waited to be deported back to Mexico. When She was deported back to Mexico she tried once again with a different coyote. This coyote helped her travel from Sonora to Tijuana. From there, She got a different coyote and they went through the border by car again. She was hiding under the car seats. With every second passing, all she did was pray uncomfortably. Prayed to be able to get through and arrive.

She was successful in getting through and after that they took her to a parking lot. The coyote and the rest of them were waiting on another coyote to take my mom to her final destination. He then came and took her to his house. They planned to take her to her flight which was at night. During the day, they fed my mom and bought her clothes since she only had what she was wearing. Time went by, and it was time for her to go to the airport. She got there with her plane ticket and a paper that had words in Spanish like salida, bano and entrada. She boarded the plane on her way to New York to meet up with her brother to ensure that they would have a better place to live than in Mexico. Days after spending time in Brooklyn, my mother and father reunited again with my uncle fAfter time passed, my dad was able to find work in the Bronx which caused my mother and father to move and find an apartment to live in. My parents journey to the U.S. was a bit crazy, but just to give me and my siblings a better life that they couldn't have.

Noelia Galindo

LGBTQ+ Rights

The LGBTQ+ is abbreviation for lesbian, gay, bisexual, transgender , queer , or questioning , intersex , asexual and more. The reason why people fight for it it's because they wanted to have the rights that a normal person would have. Like normal couples have fun dates, aren't getting hate from other people, have rights, but if it's a gay couple or a lesbian couple they would get discriminated against in stores, restaurants basically anywhere they go they would receive hate and dirty looks from other people. They wanted to have the freedom to do whatever they like to do with their future partner without a problem. The people are fighting for the rights that they don't have yet. They can get kicked out of school, jobs or denied housing. In many states they aren't allowed to get married. There was also violence meaning hate crime. Another one is parenting, meaning that they can't marry in some states you can and cannot. There's many topics about them getting discriminated against such as employment discrimination and housing discrimination. Why is my social justice issue important, it's because they have the right to date whoever they want and also get married. In different countries you would get killed if you're part of the lgbtq+ community. Not many people have the freedom to be who they are and express themself on what they are.

So LGBTQ+ are fighting for their own rights. They want to be equal just like other people. 44% of native and indigenous lgbt+ youth experienced homelessness. So they live in the streets without any family support or other people. Many youth and adults would run away from their houses due to discrimination from their own family members. They also experience harmful things such as bullying , hate comments outside and on social media and getting hit by random people. Living in the street is very dangerous for them especially when it's cold outside or raining. There can be many bugs and rats that can affect them later on. Some people gather up to protest about LGBTQ homelesses. They protested in Washington Square Park demanding more shelters from them so they can live safely and be happy with their new housing. But the mayor's office said the new budget will invest 100 new crisis shelter beds.

There's many topics about them getting discriminated against such as employment discrimination and housing discrimination. The history started in the 1960s. The event occurred in 1961 in Illions. In that time they were the first state to be discriminated against by other people. Another one is in 1969 "the stonewall inn". The stonewall was a club where everyone was allowed to be inside without getting discriminated against. Meaning queens and homeless. But on June 28 1969 (New York city) there was much police harassment, patrons, and neighborhood residents began throwing objects at the police. They were also calling them names such as pigs, cooper.Policies begin to hand-cuff people , doesn't matter whether you're drunk but one masculine dress as a woman was complaining that the police handcuffed her but tightly. Policies weren't respecting people's safety. People began to protest in the streets. They protested in time square in 1969. I wanted justice on what the police were doing to them. It wasn't fair that the policies were doing that. On June 6 2019 , policies decided to make an apology to the people who were hurt by the policies and who were discriminated against. The police commissioner James P O'nell said it was wrong what the police did. One current event is the Orlando shooting. It happened on Sunday night at the gay club in Orlando. There was a massing shooting at the gay club. Omar mateen was the one who killed 49 people at the club. Omar Mateen did not like when two men were kissing. It was heartbreaking to the LGTBQ+ community. People were scared when the gunman started to shoot at those 49 people. One of the victims said "I could just see him shooting at everyone and I can clearly hear the gunshot." He also said "and I'm just laying there and thinking , I'm next ,

I'm dead". But Omar called the police saying that he created a mass shooting at the club. He had a conversation with the police. But Omar also some of them survive but some of them lost their lives. People attended their funerals and left them flowers, candles, etc. it was sad to see the family members crying because they lost their own child due to a mass shooting at the club. The Orlando mayor Buddy Dyer said "we are dealing with something we never imagined" , "We will not be defined by the act of cowardly hater. We will be defined by how we respond , how we treat each other".

Therefore , the LGBTQ+ will protest for their rights at the end of the day. The LGBTQ+ has suffer because people would discriminated them or see them as not a human being. Everyone should be treated with respect and care. They have the right to be who they want to be and express themself. People should judge them. Like this one quote says "don't judge by its cover". It's very important for us to not be rude to them and respect their Privacy. I really hope that they treat them as one of us. My hope is to treat them with respect. And them have their own rights and have freedom to do what they like to do.

LGBQT Rights

Growing up I used to like wearing skirts, dresses, and trying on heels but I also loved playing sports and other physical activities. I found it easier and more comfortable to wear pants or stretchy clothing in order for me to have fun doing what I loved. This resulted in people thinking I was or am a lesbian or some sort of form of liking other females, even as far as thinking I wanted to identify as a boy. As I got older I continued playing sports and wearing clothes I felt the most comfortable in, therefore my wardrobe consisted of sweatpants, sweaters, and baggy clothing.

In elementary school I would play basketball with the boys in the morning and at recess. I knew I was good because they wouldn't have picked me to be on their teams if I wasn't. There would be times where I would get into arguments with certain boys in my class while playing baseball or over petty things that did not seem so petty at the time. One of these boys would call me a boy girl or say I had a skin disease because I have lighter complexion birthmarks on my face. Of course I would come back with my own remarks but being called a boy angered me but I would brush it off by thinking they would only say that because I am better than them. Considering I was around 10-12 years old, and I was starting to go through puberty, this made me question my identity in physical and mental ways. I missed weeks of school in fifth grade because I simply did not want to go. I was exhausted with people and getting u everyday to go to the one place I hated most.

I went into sophomore year of high school with a number of friends that I made from the softball team because we were allowed to play during covid in 2021 of my freshman year. The girls that I met later told me they thought I was gay or was currently gay. My reply to that comment almost every time is "Everyone thinks that," with a quick eye roll and smile to hide the annoyance in my voice. I can't help that people are curious but constantly telling me that you think I'm gay or am, is one of the most disrespectful and irritating things you can do towards me.

Last year (2022) in the winter, I went upstate to pick up my little cousin because he spent his mid winter break with our family. When we got there I was wearing a new pair of thick, baggy Nike sweatpants, my usual braids and a sweater, which is mostly an everyday look for me in the winter. A few moments after he saw me, he asked me if I was a boy. I answered no as calmly and politely as I could because he was only 4 at the time, and I didn't want to sound too aggressive. But his question made me think, if he thinks I look like a boy, what do other people think? I try not to think of this moment too much but it made me question if I should change my appearance so people can stop wondering if I'm a boy or gay or a dyke.

Last year (2022) around this time in the spring, my friend revealed to me that her dad had asked her if I was a boy, while picking her up from our softball game. I wish she never disclosed this to me because after hearing that, I wanted to be alone. This meant little kids, kids my age, and adults couldn't even tell I'm a girl. Now I was questioning more than ever, "Should I change the way I dress? Do I need to lose weight? Should I change my hair?" Right before these horrendous questions were asked, each time I would start to love myself and be comfortable in my skin.

Sometime before winter break, my friend and I were waiting in the lobby of our school and a girl I knew from the volleyball team was leaving with two of her friends. We said hi to each other and they continued to leave but the girl came back a few seconds later. She said her friend, who is a girl, thought I was cute and wanted to know if I was a dyke. I said no and sorry with a closed lip smile because of how irritated I was. Another incident where someone I knew thought I was a dyke or gay was in my school's bathroom. While washing my hands, one of my classmates asked me if I was a dyke because I always seem to be wearing sweatpants and have my hair in natural braids. That day I just so happened to be wearing sweatpants and found myself explaining it was because I had a softball game afterschool and I wanted to be able to change quickly. Which was partially true but I also found them comfortable, not that it was any of her business.

Earlier in March of this year, my friend and I went to Chipotle after softball practice, and decided to eat in the seated area near the door. A homeless guy came in a few moments after we started eating and stared at us. As he continued to stare I told him to leave us alone, and he asked if I was a boy. I was wearing skinny jeans and a puffy jacket with my hood on because it makes me warmer. I was extremely annoyed and wanted to punch this guy, but I didn't want to cause a scene especially because I hate attention. This incident got under my skin and made me vent about it in my notes app on my iphone. I would share things like "This is why I hate being around people... I rather stay single for the rest of my life than deal with slick comments... My friends are liars when they say I look good or whatever... I'm the ugliest one out of all of my friends. I think they hang out with me because they feel bad or to make them feel better about themselves."

Another inconvenience in my life is when my friends say "I would date you if you were gay." In these situations I know they're trying to joke but it's annoying and it's not even the slightest bit of funny. It feels as though they are trying to get me to announce that I am gay or bisexual when I'm not. Also when I give in and try to engage in their stupid jokes, they would say "Are you sure you are not gay?," sometimes laughing or by mumbling to where they think I can't hear them.

Although there is nothing wrong with the lgbtq, you should never assume someone's identity.

Needless to say, people should always think before they speak and consider how others feel and provokes them to create new insecurities about themselves. Girls that play sports or feel comfortable in baggy clothes should never let what people say or think cloud their minds and make them question who they are. Don't let what others say stop you from being yourself, only change what you truly want to if it makes you happier.

Chabely Gonzalez

Women's Basic Human Rights!

Women have been fighting for equality for decades. They have just been trying to strive for the same rights as men. In some states, they don't even have the right to their bodies. Women's rights are a social issue that affects women all over the world. Women need to try to advocate for their rights. When women speak up, their voices aren't heard, and people don't realize how important it is that young girls fear what they can't and can do with their bodies.

It's important to advocate for your basic human rights. Men can do whatever they want while women have been fighting since the 1800s. No one has tried to stop men from achieving what they want. Women struggle to achieve what they want, especially women of color. The system failed us from the very beginning. It was set up for men to achieve more and earn more money. Today 18 countries allow men to prohibit their wives from working. In the working industry, women are belittled and always have the mindset that men can do better than them because that's all that they were taught and knew from a young age. The article 25 Shocking Facts About The Reality Girls Face Now States, "130 million girls are denied the human right to education worldwide"(Melanie Rhodes). This is limiting humanity's potential and giving men all the power when the system doesn't even know what we are capable of.

The first-ever women's convention happened in July of 1848. It was called the Secena Falls Convention. It was a 2 day-long event. On the first day, only women were allowed to attend. It was the beginning of the women's suffrage movement. The event was set up by 5 women: Elizabeth Cady Staton, Lucretia Mott, Mary M'Clintock, Martha Coffin Wright, and Jane Hunt. Women were speaking out about their social, civil, and religious rights. Women brought up 11 resolutions. One of them was the right to vote (accomplished 10 decades later). The declaration of sentiments stated, "We hold these truths to be self-evident; that all men and women are created equal"(Stanton). Their declaration was stating ways that they could be equal to men. Their demands are things that men were given and they never needed to ask for. The women felt injustice. If they didn't fight for their rights, who would? "The declaration of sentiments was the Seneca Falls Convention's manifesto that described women's grievances and demands. Written primarily by Elizabeth Cady Stanton, it distilled the importance of the Seneca Falls Convention: for women to fight for their constitutionally guaranteed right to equality as U.S citizens."(History.com). They wrote about how unfairly they were treated by a man.

A major issue that women are facing now is that violence against them. In January of 2023, 50 women were kidnapped during the daylight in Burkina Faso. In the article Turk Alarmed At The Abduction Of At Least 50 Women In Burkina Faso "I am alarmed that dozens of women out to search for food for their families were abducted in broad daylight, in what could be the first such attack deliberately targetting women in Burkina Faso" (Volker Turk). He called for their release and for the people that adopted them to be held up accountable. They were allegedly taken by groups that were armed. A policy that helps protects women from violent acts like this is the Violence Against Women Act. "The Violence Against Women Act (VAWA) is a federal law that, in part, provides housing protections for people applying for or living in units subsidized by the federal government and who have experienced domestic violence, dating violence, sexual assault, or stalking, to help keep them safe and reduce their likelihood of experiencing homelessness"(U.S Department Of Housing And Urban Development). This law is something that women can lean on if their relationships end up putting them in danger. In some cases, it's the only thing that makes them feel safe if they have lost everyone in their life. One person that is leading the cause of protecting women is Malala Yousafzai.

Ever since she was young she has been fighting for women to be able to get an education. When she was younger she experienced not being able to go to school or even outside because the Taliban took over control of her village. Her father and she have been fighting and advocating for women's rights all over the world. She was the youngest person to win a noble Peace Prize. " I established Malala Fund, a charity dedicated to giving every girl an opportunity to achieve the future she chooses. In recognition of our work, I received the Nobel Peace Prize in December 2014 and became the youngest-ever Nobel laureate" (Malala).

Many women around the world are still advocating and speaking out against gender inequality. We need to do better for future girls in hopes they won't have to worry about going out and getting kidnapped just because of their gender or walking outside at night.

Works Cited

Yousafzai, Malala. "Malala's Story."

    Malala Fund. 2020, https://malala.org/malalas-story Accessed 28 March 2023.

Rhodes, Melanie. "25 Shocking Facts About The Reality Girls Face Now."

    One. 11 October 2018 https://www.one.org/us/blog/update-stats-gender-inequality/
 Accessed 28th March 2023.

History.com Editors "Scena Falls Convention."

    History. 19 November 2019

https://www.history.com/topics/womens-history/seneca-falls-convention Accessed 21 March 2023.

Office Of The High Commissioner For Human Rights "Türk alarmed at the abduction of at least 50 women in Burkina Faso."

United Nations. 16 January 2023 https://www.ohchr.org/en/press-releases/2023/01/turk-alarmed-abduction-least-50-women-burkina-faso Accessed 27 March 2023.

U.S. Department of Housing and Urban Development "Violence Against Women Act (VAWA)"

U.S. Department of Housing and Urban Development. 14 March 2023.

https://www.hud.gov/VAWA Accesed 27 March 2023.

Cristal Gonzalez

The History of
Women's Rights

The history of women's rights is a long and spanning centuries of struggle and progress. Women have fought for the right to vote, the right to work, and the right to be treated as equal citizens under the law. These struggles have had an extreme impact on society as a whole and they continue to form our lives today.

The women's rights movement began in the late 19th and early 20th centuries, when women began to demand the rights to vote. This movement led to the 19th amendment to the US constitution in 1920. Which granted women rights to vote. This was a major victory for women's rights. But it was only the beginning of their victory.

Another women's rights movement began in the 1960s and 1970s, when women began to demand greater equality in the workplace and in society as a whole. This movement led to the passage of laws forbidding discrimination on the basis of sex. As well as the establishment of programs to promote gender equality.

Today women continue to fight for their rights in variety of areas. Including equal pay, reproductive rights, and the right to be free from harassment and violence. While much progress has been made, there is still much work to be done to ensure that women are treated as equal citizens under the law.

In conclusion, the history of women's rights has been a long difficult story but it's been a story of progress. Women have fought for their rights for centuries, and their struggles have had an extreme impact on society as a whole. Today we continue to benefit from efforts of those who came before us, and we must continue to fight for the rights of women.

Rashida Issaka

Women's Rights

Most women and girls across the globe are still facing discrimination on the basis of sex and gender. Gender inequality underpins many problem which is disproportionately affect women and girls, such as domestic and sexual violence, low pay, lack of access to education, and inadequate healthcare.

For many years women's rights movements have fought hard to address this inequality, campaigning to change laws or talking to the streets to demand their rights are respected. And new movements have flourished in the the digital age, such as #Me Too campaign which highlights prevalence of gender based violence and sexual harassment.

During the 19th and early 20th century, people began fighting for the right of women to vote. In 1893 New Zealand became the first country to give women the right to vote on an international level. This moment grew to spread all around the world, and thanks to the efforts of everyone involved in this struggle, today women's suffrage is the right under the convention of elimination of all forms of discrimination against women.

Every woman and girl has sexual and reproductive rights. This means that they are entitled to equal access to health services like contraception and safe abortion,to choose if, when and who they marry and to decide if they want to have children and if so how many, when and with whom. Women should be able to live without fear of gender-based-violence, including rape and other sexual violence, female genetal mutilation (FGM),forced marriage, forced pregnancy, forced abortin,and forced sterilization.

Intersectional feminism is the idea that all of the reasons some might be discriminated against, including race, gender, sexual orientation, gender identity, economic class, and disability, among others, overlap, and intersect with each other. One way of understanding this would be to look at how this might apply in the real world setting, such as Dominica, where our research has shown that women sex workers,who are often people of color,or transgender, or both, suffer torture persecution by the police.

Carlos Jiminez

The Gun Violence

There are many social justice issues impacting the world today. Gun violence is one of the main issues that are still occurring until today. The people that are mostly more affected are the teachers and students in the school. People are fighting for gun control to be more safe in their community from a lost bullet and to protect their families. This issue is important because countless innocent lives have been claimed by children, fathers, mothers and even the law enforcement.

It's important to care about this issue because it consists of saving lives but also taking lives intentionally or by mistake and it becomes a problem. a loss for the dead victims' families that becomes a very big problem. there's people that are responsible with their firearms and know how to use it if any means necessary. People nowadays mostly carry a firearm to have the protection of their property or themselves as self defense against any threat that comes their way to protect their family or civilian.

The first school mass shooting happened in 1891 a 70 year old male named James Foster shot a group of students with a shotgun in the playground of St. Mary's Parochial School Newburgh New York causing minor injuries on the students. an early event that happens is the Assassination of Abraham Lincoln by john wilkes booth a famous actor assassinated Lincoln at the ford's theater. Laws like the second amendment which gave the right to a citizen to carry a firearm which became a debate of the constitution. The second amendment was firstly passed to prevent having a professional standing army in the U.S but it seemed like it wasn't intended to do that in return.

One event that happened recently was the nashville private christian elementary school shooting where a 28 year old killed three children and three adults. The shooter had drawn a map of different locations of the school including entry points of this building.it said it's the deadliest school shooting since the attack in Uvalde, texas last year. Laws that have been passed down are like the second amendment.

Finally one person or more like a uniting community of Americans named Brady campaign that goes against gun violence. They wanted to stop school shootings which are the most important issues today as well as fighting to have a control on gun violence.

In conclusion, social justice issue is something we should all care about because it affect a lot of families as well as the community that a problem like this that becomes a state issue and something that some people take as a joke or something to do or in worse cases the only option they might have because of some mental illness or mental abuse from something that happen in school or at home. I hope that in the future this issue can be controlled and changed for the good as well as the people that these guns are being selled to make a greater good in this country and in the schools.

Pride

As a little girl who grew up in a Puerto Rican Christian household, my family always made it clear to us that their love was unconditional. They would make little comments like "Well, whenever you get a boyfriend or girlfriend…" and my mom regularly asked me who I liked and made sure I knew that I didn't have to hide if I was gay. This is because in the news, we would see people were harassed and even killed because of who they loved, and although they knew they couldn't protect us from that, they could raise us right. My parents always made sure we knew that the daily discrimination that members of the LGBTQ+ community faced wasn't okay. I grew up very sheltered from the idea that anyone was made to feel wrong for who they love or who they are. I never had any idea of LGBTQ+ discrimination until I was about 9 years old.

I grew up watching crime shows, and I always thought it was entirely fictional, but when a family friend whom I knew as a baby was suddenly killed in front of her building by her own brother, I realized how crazy crimes unfolded in the real world, too. It turned out that she was killed over her sexual orientation. Then is when I truly started to see how clear it was, and how incredibly dangerous it was to just be who you are. I started to notice how badly kids were being bullied for being LGBTQ+ or how it was an insult to call someone gay. As a result of this, it created fear in me, despite my entire families effort to make sure I never felt that way. The belief that my family worked so hard to instill in me seemed to disappear, and the fear of the outside world soon became all I felt. I look back now, and I know I was gay ever since I was a little girl. But because of the fear I had (and still do), I didn't tell anyone until I was 17 years old. That fear I felt was a fear most (if not all) LGBTQ+ members feel constantly and have to live with that fear every day.

According to the Trevor Project's research, as of last year, over 45% of LGBTQ+ youth seriously considered suicide in the past year, and 14% of LGBTQ youth attempted suicide in the past year. That fear can cause real anxiety and depression, having to lie and hide who you are takes a toll on your mental state, as it did to mine. As of last year, over 73% of LGBTQ youth reported experiencing symptoms of anxiety and 58% of LGBTQ youth reported experiencing symptoms of depression. This fear though, where did it come from? As it turned out, the research also showed that about 1 out of 10 violent victimizations against LGBTQ+ people are hate crimes. When I see these statistics, the fear I have feels validated.

When it comes to religious groups, some religious families even go as far as sending their children to conversion therapy. It was found that 13% of LGBTQ+ youth reported being subjected to conversion therapy, with 83% reporting it occurred when they were under age 18. There is no credible research that suggests that conversion therapy is effective or even useful, and it is actually harmful to LGBTQ+ patients and can contribute to lifelong trauma. The fear of homosexuality, or homophobia, has been around for a while, and this fear causes people to seek drastic measures simply because of those who don't understand or accept their loved ones for who they are, as they are.

I was lucky enough to grow up with an accepting family, but still the judgment and hatred from the outside world was enough to instill a sense of fear in me that I still have yet to shake. There isn't just fear of judgment or assault, but even death. Many members of the lgbtq+ community have been killed because they were LGBT. It isn't ok nor fair that people lose their lives or live in a constant state of fear due to who they love or who they are. There should be no anxiety or hesitation in coming out to anyone. I should have never gotten to that point which is why changing how this world treats the lgbtq+ community is necessary.

Wendy Mejia

Climate Change

There are many social justice issues impacting the world today. One problem that people are trying to address is reducing carbon emissions and the burning of fossil fuels like coal, oil and gas. Climate change are long term shifts in temperatures and weather patterns. Some of these shifts may be natural or caused by human activities that have been the main reason for climate change. It impacts people who live in areas that are vulnerable to coastal storms, drought, sea level rise, those who live in poverty, older adults and immigrant communities. People are fighting to help because climate change worsens over time. This issue is important because some people do not believe in climate change or think climate change is real. This became a problem and will continue to affect us now and future generations.

It's important to care about climate change because people tend to not realize how climate change is real and is affecting the earth on a daily basis due to our human activity. The world today is getting hotter every day due to all the carbon emissions that get released into the air from the burning of fossil fuels. One data points that in 2023, there's been many deaths due to sea rise levels that cause tornadoes, floodings, hurricanes, etc. This impacts communities who are poor or facing poverty in most developing countries since they don't have the resources or the financial help to get out from where they live. Another data point that concerns this issue is greenhouse gasses. Greenhouse gasses occur when gasses in the earth's atmosphere are trapped in the sun's heat. They create heat islands. Heat islands are caused by lack of space due to many buildings being close together and carbon emissions being trapped in. New York is considered to be a heat island. This means that people won't be able to handle extreme heat leading to 700 deaths per year. If the issue is not addressed, then the damages would be done and there will not be a way to reverse it. Time is the only thing that we do not have, if we don't take action now then we never will.

There have been many different events that led to how climate change was discovered and how it will get worse over time. One event that happened in this issue's history was the discovery of rising global temperatures in 1938. During this event, an amateur scientist named Guy Callender recorded global temperatures and realized the world has gotten hotter and risen over time (50 years). Other scientists did not believe that humans could impact a large system such as the climate. This event impacted the issue by the discovery that the global temperatures were rising in 1938 due to carbon emissions being released which meant it was a problem not only for a specific place but worldwide with negative consequences. Svante Arrhenius impacted the issue of climate change . He was a Swedish scientist who claimed in 1896 that fossil fuel combustion may eventually result in enhanced global warming. He wanted to prove and show the cause of the different glaciations that the planet had gone through throughout its history. Many scientists did not believe him but he wanted to prove the influence of human activity on climate change which supported his theory/ predictions. He wanted to determine the factor for these climatic events which could have been carbon dioxide in the earth's atmosphere as atmospheric gasses which also cause greenhouse effects. He received the 1903 nobel prize for chemistry for the theories that nobody really knew about or where it would be placed in order to be said in the world. He founded a new field of research: physical chemistry which helped other scientists find solutions to how climate change occurs. (UK Research and Innovation) For instance, how carbon dioxide and greenhouse gasses affect the atmosphere due to human activity. Many did not care because it was not affecting them physically until another event that impacted the issue in October 1948, Donora, PA. They experienced severe respiratory or cardiovascular problems, it was difficult for them to breathe and the death toll nearly rose to 40. Air pollution has become a harsh consequence of industrial growth in the country and world. This made awareness on how air pollution is one of the main factors of climate change that affected many people which led to many deaths. Due to this event, they were able to at least try and take control over air pollution with regulations being made in order to reduce air pollution. Many laws have been passed that have impacted climate change because many people did not know how it was affecting them but president Nixon did. He passed on the Clean Air Act to reduce fossil fuel production due to carbon emissions being released into the earth. (United States Environmental Protection Agency) These events and policies are being made to help us humans survive since heat waves are causing the world to heat up. Climate change overall can't be reversible if we don't act now because time is all we have left.

One event that influenced climate change was the Syria drought that happened in April 2021. During this event, Syria faced one of the worst droughts that it has seen in seven decades.(Lyall & Shaar) They faced many conflicts due to the drought because they didn't have any food and they were depending on their crops. Droughts are an effect that climate change brings due to the hot weather and temperatures. This event did not only make progress on climate change by bringing awareness of what one of the consequences could be if we don't take actions into what we are doing to the atmosphere but it brought more awareness with the contribution of other countries to reduce carbon emissions and bring the world to net zero emissions. Our actions define what is going to happen to future generations if we keep on releasing carbon emissions, greenhouse gasses, air pollution, etc.

Al Gore used the Syria drought as an example of what climate change can cause. Gore was the 45th vice president of the United States who discussed the challenges that the world is facing right now world wide. Climate change is a topic that people aren't aware of and still unknown. He prioritized the climate crisis and organized the first hearing on man made global warming in 1981. (Roberta Annan) He made a document about climate change in the early 2000s in order to tell the truth to billions of people. People called him crazy for believing and getting involved in such a topic as climate change which people believed that climate change should even be a priority because there's been worse "problems" being faced. Al Gore releases an American documentary film named " An Inconvenient Truth" based on his traveling lecture tour on the human challenge of climate change. It brought many people to gather from different societies and across multiple countries to work towards the main challenges. It helped to promote more activists to fight against the appeal of Trump discarding the Paris agreement. This was part of why the Paris Agreement influenced climate change. This agreement was for all the members of the UN climate change conference in Paris (196 parties) that signed this agreement to reduce global greenhouse gas emissions and provide financial help to developing countries to fight climate change. Developing countries are the ones being the most affected from many floods, hurricanes, tornadoes, etc. When they want to contribute and make their country better, due to the many natural disasters being made, they can't and they have to start from zero. This change was impactful because it brought more awareness with the contribution of other countries to reduce carbon emissions and bring the world to net zero emissions. It made climate change a priority and hoped to spread awareness to others about climate change with further solutions to these challenges.

In conclusion, climate change is something we should all care about and be a priority. It's important to care about climate change because it will affect us eventually either now or closer than we think it is. Many policies and acts are being made in order to reduce the damage being made and limit the amount of harm we are causing to the environment. In the future, we hope to get more people to believe and be more aware of the climate crisis. Our voice matters, climate change matters.

Melanie Mella Castillo

Immigration

"Nos vamos a mudar para Nueva York," is something I remember hearing my mom or different family members say at our house in the Dominican Republic. I remember the whole process. Going to different offices and places I didn't understand. My mom once said that our biological father wanted us to move to NYC, but I didn't really understand.

"¿Que era Nueva York?" I'd think to myself. Going from 6 to 7 years old, I didn't really understand much about there being different places besides what I already knew -my neighborhood in DR, my school, my grandmother's house- much less an entire country.

After speaking with my mother about it, she told me that our biological father was a citizen of this country and wanted us to live with him. I guess I never really understood why until I was a bit older. What I didn't get was why we were leaving our lives in DR behind for someone we never saw. The days leading up to our flight here were a blur.

People saying their goodbyes in different settings. "La extrañare mucho vecina/o" or "Te quiero mucho mi niña," were common phrases I'd hear.

November 14, 2012, came around and I still didn't acknowledge that we were going to a different country. The concept of there being another country or place was so mind-boggling to me, nevertheless, at that young age, I chose to ignore it. I remember getting to the airport and they told me I had to go and leave my family behind. From my aunt to my cousin to my uncle and the taxi driver. The panic set in and I began bawling. As I looked around, I seemed to be the only one having this reaction along with my mom's occasional tear that I knew she was trying to hide with the yellow sunglasses she was wearing.

I'd hear her trying to calm me down, saying things like, "Regresaremos a Santo Domingo en unos días mi amor. Vas a volver a ver a tus tios y primos," in a voice that brought me comfort.

Something I kept close to me was the necklace that Francisco, the taxi driver, gave me; a necklace with a pendant con La Virgen Maria. He was a very close family friend who I knew I'd miss very much. As we boarded the plane, I could feel myself a bit calmer than before, with the promise that I'd be going back home in a few days. I sat with my stepfather throughout the flight and watched as the woman next to me freaked out a bit due to her fear of heights I assume, or the occasional small talk. I remember when we finally landed, it was a cold night at JFK, significantly different from the weather that I was used to. The cold air was blowing on my face as we were walking to the car.

I started school about a week after we got here. It was confusing to hear people talk in a language I didn't understand. It sounded as if they were speaking in gibberish. Or the way that they were dressed in these jackets for the cold. I'd think about how in DR I would be wearing my gray uniform shirt tucked in and navy blue pants with a black belt. It was proper school attire. Here they'd wear this light blue uniform shirt with any color pants or no student in my class would wear a uniform. Starting in the second grade was a bit of a challenge. I didn't know anyone and I hated how I had to be separated from the rest of the class just because I didn't speak English. After a while, I did learn the language and I was able to make friends. That didn't stop me from being held back, however.

The new school year started and I was repeating the grade, without my friends or anyone I knew in general. A few days later the girl I would call my best friend for the remainder of elementary school walked in. Salma and her family had just moved from Cuba to the United States. I was fast to befriend her and asked her how she was doing. She told me that she was a bit scared and that she didn't know the language. I was able to relate to her story and experience with moving to a new environment. Hence why it was so easy for us to become friends.

I never really thought about how I was an immigrant though, mainly because it wasn't really a topic of conversation for an elementary school kid. That was all up until the 4th grade, when this boy who was our other best friend, said something to me and Salma during after-school dismissal.

"I can do something that neither of you can when I'm 18."

"What's that?" I asked.

"I can vote and you guys can't because you're immigrants."

Those words stayed with me for the remainder of the day. As I got home I asked my mom about what he said. She explained to me that that wasn't the case and he just didn't know what he was talking about. That's when I learned that if one or both of your parents are citizens of this country, that makes you a citizen despite of what country you were born in. Still with this knowledge, I began to imagine how it was for other immigrants. At this age, I was oblivious to the hardships of many immigrants. In class, my 4th-grade teacher asked me, "Why did your parents come to this country?"

"To get better opportunities," I replied.

"Precisely. Many people come to this country to get a better education, better quality of life, and better opportunities for their families including their children," she said.

This was all part of the lesson we were learning that day and the day I started to become aware that it wasn't the same for many immigrants, or that they still kept referring to immigrants as aliens but they weren't from outer space. The process I went through, those offices or places I didn't understand; they didn't go through the same thing. Fast forwarding to the 7th grade, I was in Ms. Mendia's Spanish class. We had a project where we were supposed to write an essay about DREAMers. In this project, we were assigned a "person" and wrote about their immigration story. The person I got was a Venezuelan woman who was against DREAMers getting certain opportunities because she went through the entire immigration process. I remember she believed that it was unfair that she had to work for these opportunities, while they were basically getting them for free.

I went home that day to talk to my dad about this project. He explained to me that some people believed things like the Dream Act shouldn't exist. I was able to learn that the Dream Act would let undocumented immigrants stay in the United States if they're able to qualify for it, more specifically young immigrants. I wrote the essay for a grade but it just didn't feel right to write an essay supporting an argument that would make it harder for immigrants; more challenging than it already is.

As of 2023, almost 2.3 million immigrants are on the path to obtaining U.S. citizenship through the Dream Act. The vast majority of DREAMers come to America at a very young age meaning they grow up in this country, making it all they know. The Dream Act would provide a permanent solution allowing them to stay in this country. Generally speaking, if the Dream Act were to be removed, a large portion of immigrants in this country would be facing deportation in a country that they may not know.

Immigrants in the United States face countless challenges. They are facing discrimination or the denial of certain services. It's worse for undocumented immigrants. They're faced with deportation, being separated from their children, and high poverty rates as they're not eligible for benefits, etc. What many American people fail to realize is that immigrants contribute to the economy of the United States. We make up a large part of the workforce in this country, oftentimes going unnoticed or blending in with the crowd. At least that's how my experience has been living in New York City. The diversity, music, food, communities, and languages that we see here in this city are due to immigrants coming in from different parts of the world. It's a beautiful thing really. Most importantly, we are not from outer space.

Noceda Si Se Dio

My mother was born on October 27 1983, in a small pueblo called Hueyapan in the state of Morelos in Mexico, to Fransico Noceda and Leonisa Espinosa, and they named my mother Cristela Noceda Espinosa. She was one of 12 children that my grandparents would have. My grandparents were honest farm workers, by the time my mother was born 2 children had already died, one boy on his 2nd birthday fell sick and died, a few days after his death his beloved dog also died. Tragedy also struck when her soon to be baby sister died at birth. My mother at 15 years of age left her hometown and went to work in Cuernavaca, a small city with more middle- class families. She followed the steps of her sisters and worked as a maid, in which she was paid around $500 pesos every 15 days. Housing was given to her and oftentimes her bosses were "relajados''. Just one time in which she accidentally used a metal scrub to scrub down an oven in which she got in trouble. The lady was overall a bully and my mom ended up calling her sister Emma to go pick her up as she could not see herself working in that toxic household. The first of my family to leave Mexico and go to El Norte was my aunt Emma just in time to witness 9/11. She described hearing louds sirens that day, something that she was not used to hearing. Filled with panic and anxiety she called her husband or what i consider my first father, "tio pilar" but due to high traffic that day the call never entered. It was not until she turned on the Tv to see that the twin towers had been hit, something she took a while to process. Meanwhile back in mexico my mother was working when all of sudden the tv stations were interrupted with a breaking news broadcast. To get the narrative straight i asked my mother "cómo te enteraste de 9/11" her response was "fue temprano la mañana que estaba haciendo el desayuno de la señora cuando me llamó que vaya en su cuarto porque algo malo pasó en nueva york. Ella sabía que mi hermana estaba aquí, y me dijo que podía usar el teléfono para llamarla. La traté varias veces y no pude comunicarme con ella. Entre su cuarto y las primeras imágenes que tenían en la tele estaba la torre norte lleno de humo, y en unos segundos yo vi como la torre sur también saco humo. Me quedé un rato con la señora hasta que cayó la primera torre, se podía ver la gente como caída de las torres y en la tele se veía como la gente corría. Me dio más miedo cuando la otra torre cayó y empezaban a hablar de un posible ataque terrorista y pláticas de una tercera guerra, pero yo más preocupada por mi hermana porque no podía comunicarse y no sabia bien donde vivía." This was a hardship for many that day that tried contacting any family member living in New York City, the phone lies were jammed. But 9/11 didn't stop my mother from thinking about going to the US. The only thing stopping her was waiting for her sister Luisa to go along with her brother Silvino. To get the best narrative of what inspired my mom to go to the US and what she had to go through I thought it was best to just ask her. The following is in Spanish but will be broken down as we go along. "Cuéntame de tu historia, cómo cruzaste la frontera y que te motivó?"

Me sentí inspirada porque mis hermanas decían que aquí se gana mejor y podía ganar más dinero trabajando menos, y mi idea fue trabajar para ayudar a mi familia en México. (most people living in Mexico choose to leave because of economic opportunity in the U.S. my mother felt inspired by her sisters who were in the U.S as they talked about easily making money and having safety there)Vivíamos en una casa de adobe, y quería que hagan una casa mejor. En marzo de 2004 empecé mi camino hacia el norte. Mi hermana Luisa me prestó $4,000 para llegar a los estado unidos. Salí de mi casa una madrugada fría hacia la ciudad de México, ahí tomamos un vuelo para llegar a la frontera. El vuelo me gustó, fue la primera vez que me subí. Llegamos a un hotel en la frontera de México y esperamos ahí dos días. Dos días porque necesitábamos un día listo y teníamos que prepararnos con comida y agua para el viaje. No tenía mucho miedo, me sentía feliz y emocionada. Una noche nos dijeron que ya estábamos listos, solo llevamos comida, nada de ropa ni cosas de material. Caminamos toda una noche en la madrugada los guías nos dejaron en un cerca y dijeron que nos tenían que dejar ahí y que los esperabamos. La razón fue porque necesitaban más agua porque ya no alcanzaba. Nos pidieron nuestros dinero para comprarlo y se fueron. En la noche escuchábamos cómo unos lobos hacían su llanto, al principio fue uno, luego dos, y cada vez se escuchaban más. Mi tío y otro hombre dijeron que teníamos que actuar rápido. Agarramos palos de árboles y usando un encendedor hicimos una fogata.Al amanecer no llegaron y no podíamos quedarnos ahí porque hacía mucho frío. Tuvimos que salir y caminar cuando de repente apareció una camioneta. Se detuvo y se bajaron unos hombres y nos pidieron nuestra información. Nombre y que hacíamos, quieran una explicación porque estabamos ahi. (con mi tío, 4 conocidos de pueblo. En total éramos como 12 (yo incluido) y me puse muy nerviosa y entonces nos subieron a la camioneta, nos dijeron que tenían que llevarnos a un centro de detención. Al llegar al centro de detención nos tomaron las huellas, nuestra fotos y nos quitaron nuestras pocas cosas que teníamos. Estando adentro nos separaron entre sexos y yo tenía miedo porque no veía a mi tío. Estando ahí escuche otras historias de mujeres que tenían meses intentando cruzar y no lo habían logrado. Muchas estaban desesperadas. Entonces ahí fue que yo me empecé a sentir muy triste y desesperado, me invadió la soledad y me puse a llorar extrañando a mi papá y mi mama. No se me olvida las galletitas que nos dieron para comer, eran saladas rellenas de crema de cacahuate y un juguito de naranja. Es difícil olvidar porque lo comí porque realmente tenía hambre. Me asomaba por una pequeña ventana para ver si veía a mi tío, porque a pesar que estaba con una vecina que estaba conmigo, tenía miedo que a mi tío lo dejaran ir sin mi. En la noche nos sacaron de ahí y nos dejaron en una gasolinera y mi tío llamó por teléfono para hacer una llamada.(In March of 2004 my mother started her journey to cross the border after being lent $4000 usd which was around 45,000 pesos. Eventually mother was caught at the border after her group was left by the guides. In 2004 alone the U.S. Border patrol apprehended a little over a million people on the southwestern border.) Despúes mandaron a buscarnos y regresamos al hotel en donde estábamos. Esa misma noche volvimos a intentar a cruzar con un guía, esta vez lo logramos. No sin antes pasar dos noches y dos días caminando entre cerros y montañas. Pasando mucho frío que nos metimos en bolsas de basura y estábamos juntos como un grupo para no pasar frío. Escuchábamos ruidos de animales raros en las noches, no sabíamos que era y nos daba miedo. Las dos experiencias más aterradoras que tuve fue cuando me separé del grupo, no se como paso y fue en medio de la noche. No veía a nadie y no escuchaba a nadie, en realidad todo duró como uno o dos minutos pero para mi fue una eternidad. No se podía ver nada, fue la cosa más oscura que viví, me llamaba tio, tio, y pensé que aquí me iban a dejar no podía ver nada y estaba perdida. Escuché despúes la voz de mi tío llamándome pero no me podía ver hasta que le seguía a su voz hasta encontrarnos otra vez. La otra experiencia fue cuando escuchamos que unos helicópteros nos empezaron a rodear. Nos escondimos junto a un árbol y también unos caballos se escuchaban y unos perros. Los guías nos decían que nadie se moviera y que no hagamos ruido porque estábamos en una zona de peligro donde había mucha vigilancia, usaban perros para detenernos, y que si corríamos soltaban a los perros. Tenía mucho miedo porque temía que nos atraparan pero más miedo que soltaran a los perros y que nos atacaban. Según los guías esto fue muy común para la guardia fronteriza. My mother's story of crossing the border is one of the things that makes me realize she is the strongest person I know. There has not been someone braver, stronger, and cooler than my mother. To be able to survive after being abandoned in the mountains with no water or food and still be able to continue your journey. Or how she managed to not let herself be discouraged after being sent to a detention center. Or how she managed to find the strength to cross the border again after being threatened with prison time as well as being physically tired of walking with no sleep. My mother managed to do it. And coming to the United states she quickly realized how life was different here. In 2005 the US unemployment rate was at a low 4% so she easily managed to find a job, the same job she would keep for 13 years.

Valore mucho el poder encontrar trabajo en una factoría de frutas y verduras porque no necesitaba hablar inglés ni estudios. A diferencia de México, para poder trabajar en una fábrica así, necesitabas un diploma de estudios o una certificación que mínimo estudiaste la secundaria o la universidad. Yo solo estudié hasta la primaria. My mom explained to me that finding a job in the US was easy, unlike in Mexico where to find a good job one needed to have a higher education. And the higher education needed would be a high school diploma, which is something that she never got the chance to have. My mother only finished elementary school and quickly had to start working to support the family. In Mexico only 63 percent of the population has a higher education above secondary. Compare that to the United States which has over 50 percent of the general population with a College degree. My mother pays taxes with an ITIN number which is similar to a SSN as it allows one to pay taxes to the IRS. except an ITIN number is only given to non resident aliens. Many estimates estimate that there are around 11 million undocumented people in the United states in 2023, and in 2015 the IRS reported 4.35 million tax returns that were filed using ITIN numbers. Furthermore in 2019, 492 Billion dollars were paid in taxes by undocumented immigrants. Now when put into perspective of the general population, the US percent of citizens who pay taxes is 59.9%. The percentage of undocumented immigrants who pay taxes is between 50-75 percent. Overall undocumented immigrants like my mother are honest workers who I think deserve to have a chance of citizenship. She, like many others, just wanted to live in a safer country, one where they could have children which would be allowed to grow up worry free. One where they could make money and like financially stable lives. I was raised by my young single mother who taught me to be grateful for what I had and to be grateful for the country. As a result I sometimes feel connected to the US in the sense that I'm thankful for all the opportunities it gave my family. Although it was not perfect, such as my mother working in the same company for over 10 years yet not being able to rise through the ranks or pay, it was still something. It was something that allowed her to put food on the table, something that allowed her to send money back to Mexico to build her house, something that allowed her to make a name for herself and the family. She managed to defy our last name and be able to say "si se dio"

Kilian Ogowan

Why Is Gun Violence
A Problem?..

What is gun violence? Well gun violence is a common global issue and is a leading cause of premature death in the U.S. Guns kill more than 38,000 people and cause nearly 85,000 injuries each year according to reporters from Wayne State University who show their insight on gun violence. Many are familiar with this issue because it has impacted many Americans and people outside the US as well for many years. My overall analysis and personal relation on the issue is that gun violence has increased dramatically because of most homicide cases throughout the years. And it is known that gun violence has been one of the biggest elements which threaten both personal safety and national security in the United States. And the personal connection I can make with gun violence is is because gun violence along with criminal justice often leaves many of my people dead or in prison and ruins many lives. Many people who are victims of gun violence are left dead while attackers are sent to prison for making dumb decisions. Even the ones with authority that possess guns tend to be left dead or have to kill another being to defend themself or protect others. Many of these deaths cause mental problems within the families of the deceased which is a sad thing to think about. But the most common and known solution would be to reduce the access of weapons and guns because it's a fact that guns are powerless without someone holding them. But this solution is easier said than done and many events in American history concerning gun violence show why this statement is true.

Past events in America were both the Easter Sunday massacre of March 30, 1975 and the walk of death of Labor Day, 1949. The Easter Sunday massacre is known to be a horrid event after the perpetrator would shoot and kill his mother, brother, sister-in-law, and eight nieces and nephews in five minutes before calling police and being arrested later. While the walk of death is known in American history as being one of the first mass shootings in the country. The suspect walked through his neighborhood for some time and started shooting and ended up killing thirteen individuals including three children, and injuring three. Thankfully the shooter was later arrested after catching the attention of the authority. Most people, including myself, believe that the introduction of the 2nd amendment of 1791 would play a part in all these horrific events to take place. The 2nd amendment the amendment that declared that the people may have arms/weapons for their defense suitable to their condition, and as allowed by law. This policy would change society and their ability to defend themselves. But the more the years went on the more these weapons became more dangerous and the more people would use them for malicious intent. A policy that tried to suppress the use of guns was the sullivian Act 1911. This act is considered a controversial gun control law in the state of New York. It dates to 1911, and is one of the older gun control laws in the United states. A fact is that the Sullivan Act required licenses for New Yorkers to have permission to own guns that are small enough to be hidden or concealed. After the act came about the sucide rate went down but unfortunately the murder rate would go up. But besides these policies and events I believe that the major event/policy that impacted the issue of gun violence was definitely the introduction of the 2nd amendment. Unfortunately this law/policy caused more bad than good in America. Although many people after the amendment came to place, were able to defend themselves and were allowed to carry firearms, it's a fact that these weapons back then weren't as lethal as they are in recent years and these newer weapons were used to kill many, injure many, and put many in jail. Many events in the world, specifically America showed why guns cause many issues and people misusing them doesn't help whatsoever.

One major event in history that could show the tragic reality that guns are an issue is The Palm Sunday massacre which was a mass-murder in 1984 Brooklyn, New

York, that led to the deaths of a total of 10 people, two women, two teenage girls, and six children one of the women was six month pregnant. Although there was one survivor, an infant girl that was found lying on the floor covered in blood, she would be adopted and taken care of. But although she was an infant and unaware of the things going on, losing people at such a young age due to gun violence must be an horrid thing to live with later on, this event was one to remember and left many scarred and scared. And the thing that angered people even more and broke their hearts was that the killer was sentenced to 32 years in prison instead of life or getting a death penalty. And him being released after those years angered people due to his intentions of killing those innocent individuals and leaving the poor girl without these same people that he killed. Overall we can see that the 2nd amendment kept following people throughout history and possibly caused this due to the ability to bear arms. And it left these innocent people and many more be-fore and after them would be killed due to gun violence which shows the issue with the amendment and guns in general. Something was needed to be done to save the lives of Aamericans, which is where lyndon b johnson would come to place. Lyndon B Johnson was the vice president in 1961 till 1963 he was promoted president of the united states after the tragic death of president john F kennedy who was previously the president. He impacted the issue by signing the Ggun Ccontrol Aact of 1968 in that year after seeing the issue of people with unlicensed weapons going around and killing or injuring people left and right including people like john F kennedy, Martinmarthur luther king, and other important figures.

This outraged lyndon so in 1968 that was when he demanded congressional ac-tion. He would later be able to sign the act which had its effect on America which was an example of this person fighting for change. Furthermore the 1968 law was a victory won for gun-control activists who prayed for a change, while many others were disappointed it didn't include a registry of firearms or federal licensing requirements for gun owners. Overall this change was able to reduce the easy access of firearms. It banned interstate shipments of firearms and ammunition to individuals and sales of guns to minors, drug addicts and people who are incompetent. It was also studied that less guns causes less death and injuries to gun violence which was good results that came out of the act. But many believed that the act was necessary because it took aways the ability of self de-fense, safety, hunting and does not prevent crimes, sales of weapons, and sucide, and it was also stated that most people's death don't come from gun violence. But lyndon B johnson was a determined man and made sure that the act would take action in america and with the help of many activist, and important figures who supported the act, the acts effect would have a more positive effect and save more lives rather than a negative one. it is to be know that the negatives were still present just less significant. But I believe in recent years times have changed and these negatives have become worse and worse. But president Lyndon's efforts can't be ignored when talking about gun violence and gun control.

Futher more in recent years it is known that his efforts had a good effect but gun violence wasn't fully done occuring in America and two events show that. The Stoneman douglas high school shooting of february 14 ,2018 where an expelled student entered Parkland, Florida's Marjory Stoneman Douglas High School and opened fire, killing 17 people and wounding 17 others, in what became at the time the deadliest shooting at a high school in United States history. And the Robb elementary shooting of May 23 2022 where a teen gunman Ramos (the suspect) allegedly purchased two assault rifles just days after turning 18 and used them to carry out the school shooting all within a span of eight days, authorities said. Nineteen children and two adults were killed in a shooting at Robb Elementary School in Uvalde County on May 24. It Was one of the many incidents relating to gun violence which took the lives of many. not to mention the Sandy Hook Elementary School shooting. where in the year 2012 is a single gunman that killed 20 1st graders and 6 educators at the school in Newtown, Connecticut. 20 of the victims were children between six and seven years old, and the other six were adult staff members. Earlier that day, before making his way to the school, the gunman had shot and killed his mother at their Newtown home. The gunman would aslo later die to suicide, shooting himself in the head. The sad part is these same kids who died that day should be sitting in 11th grade classrooms, planning for their future after their high school graduation and figuring out all the possibilities ahead. But instead their desks are as empty as the parents' hearts after the loss of their childrens and seeing such a corrupted mind go with the idea to go to an elementary school and not only shoot the mother who birthed him but several innocent children. The fear of guns in Connecticut was really in the air after this event. This shooting was able to promote the debate on gun control in the US, including the idea to make the background-check system more universal, and banning the sale and manufacture of certain types of semi-automatic firearms and magazines which can hold more than ten rounds of ammunition. This is to prevent people from getting a hold of such dangerous weapons and suddenly lose all sanity and kill the innocent. Overall this event was a good wake up call for many people and opened their eyes to the dangers of firearms and how gun control laws are necessary to keep the youth safe including the adults and seniors.

It is known that many laws/policies that took place before the event in the 2000s which were the Tiahrt Amendment of 2003 which Prohibited the ATF from publicly releasing data showing where criminals purchased their firearms and stipulated that only law enforcement officers or prosecutors could access such information.The amendment/

law effectively shielded retailers from lawsuits, academic study and the public investigations. Which I feel puts a shield on manufacturers and they would feel safer selling the weapons in question. The Tiahrt Amendments also prohibited the states from requiring gun dealers to submit inventories to law enforcement. According to many, repealing these amendments would help solve gun crimes. Along with the Protection of Lawful Commerce in Arms Act of 2005 where The Act was signed by President George W. Bush to stop all gun manufacturers from being named in federal or state civil suits by those who were victims of crimes involving guns made by that company. The act was able to prohibit causes of action against manufacturers, distributors, dealers, and importers of guns, weapons or ammunition products, and their trade associations, for the harm solely due to the criminal or unlawful misuse of firearm products or ammunition products by others when the product functioned as intended. It was also able to dismiss pending cases on October 26, 2005. But all thought it wasn't able to fully stop gun violence leading to deaths, and jail time, it prevented the innocent manufacturers from being accountable for the crimes. These laws/policies were a decent start to save lives and prevent individuals from going to prison and ruining their lives for no reason. And George W Bush signing the Protection of Lawful Commerce in Arms Act of 2005 was one of his many contributions to his gun control pursuit area while he was in office.

More on this important figure and his actions and contribution in the 2000s are that this person was the 43rd president of the united states and he would support the pursuit of gun control due to the evident rise in gun issues spreading all over America which was very impactful for many families. In other word he himself supported several gun control measures and vowed to sign a renewal of the Assault Weapons Ban if it was to reach his desk, his administration saw several advancements of gun rights on the federal level, especially in the court. he would give prosecutors the resources they needed to aggressively enforce the gun laws and will provide further funding for aggressive gun law enforcement programs. President Bush believed the ''instant check system'' was the best way to keep criminals from buying weapons at gun shows and supports any changing federal law to give gun show sponsors any type of special access to the ''National Instant Check System'' to conduct checks on the behalf of non-licensed vendors and distributors. Bush also supported raising the age from 18 to 21 to possess a handgun without parental supervision. This law would make sure that a person must be 21 or older to purchase a handgun. President Bush also supported the voluntary efforts to equip all weapons, more specifically handguns with child safety locks on them. He had stated that if the Congress passed a legislation requiring mandatory trigger safety lock for all new handguns, he would be eager to sign it. He also wanted to make sure to provide federal matching funds to make child safety locks available for every handgun in America. It is to be known that Bush supported the extending of the current known ban on high-capacity ammunition clips to include those imported from the foreign countries. He also proposed then signed legislation requiring automatic jail time for any juveniles who carried a firearm illegally or committed a crime/crimes with a gun.   Thanks to the support of president Bush, violent crime had decreased 20% percent while overall crime decreased 14% percent. Not to mention, violent juvenile crime had decreased 44% percent and overall juvenile crime by 17% percent which was the first decline in over a decade at that time which was good results and progress according to the office of justice which recognizes his help concerning the issue . He also effectively abolished parole for violent offenders, thanks to the source from the office of justice i was able to discover that violent criminals in Texas are now serving over 90 percent of their sentences while violent sex offenders are serving 100 percent of their sentences. All thanks to George Bush's efforts during these hard times where gun violence was everywhere and gun control was needed. Overall his involvement was necessary for America to prevent losing more lives.

In conclusion, gun violence has been an issue back then and is still an issue in recent years and if we want to keep our parents, our childrens, our friends, and our loved ones in general we must commit to solutions that will finally keep guns off the streets and allow people that can use them properly and keep people from falling victim to the violence and prevent aggressors in possession of weapons from ruining their lives and making dumb decisions with these weapons and end up in prison or dead. Many solutions are in the air and if the higher ups and people with a respectful voice show their support like the important figures I talked about, we can get a wider range of individuals that will try to fight for a change and help protect the people of America and even all around the world.

Nati Yuliana Paulino

Protect People Not GUNS!

There are many social justice issues impacting the world today. One problem that people are trying to address is gun violence. Gun violence is an issue that has caused many problems everywhere and has impacted many people. People are fighting to stop gun violence because it's hurting many innocent people and it's usually the ones with mental health. This issue is important because if we can stop gun violence or have more secure places we can also accomp-lishg other things that are going on around the world.

It's important to care about gun violence because too many tragedies have happened, people were killed with guns and also have ended their lives committing suicide using guns. One data point that concerns this issue is that in " 2022, 16.5 million guns were bought in America, showing how many guns are being used across the country" (Brownlee). Another data point that concerns this issue is that in "2022 there were 248 mass shootings that happened. The worst shooting happened on May 24th, 2022, when a gunman entered Robb Elementary in Uvalde, Texas and killed 19 children and two teachers" (Holland). This impacts Americans all over the country and parents who have kids attending school because now worry about their kids attending school and thinking if they are even coming back home. to even think if they feel safe in their own environment

One major event that impacted the issue of gun violence when they shot Abraham Lincoln in the theater April 15, 1865. He was the president from March 4th ,1861 to April 15th 1865. He was in Ford's theater watching " Our American cousin" in Washington DC and was shot by John Wilkes Booth with a 5.87 inch derringer on the back of his head. This event impacted the issue of gun violence because back then presidents did not have mch security and now presidents have many security to protect them of anything and when they appear somewhere people have to get checked for guns or any other weapons that can be targeted at the president or anyone else. Another event that impacted the issue of gun violence was Texas Tower gun sniper A mass shooting that took place in Austin Texas on August 1rst , 1966 Charles Whitman killed 14 people and 31 were hospitalized when a student and former Marine opened fire from the University of Texas clock tower. Many laws have been passed that have impacted the lives of many people ever since the second amendment was passed in 1789. The second amendment states " the right of the people to keep and bear Arms.." which means that people are allowed to own guns. Many mass shootings have happened ever since and even before but it's gotten to the point where teenagers own guns and are killing young kids. This has made a big impact on people but people think that as an American they have to own a gun. Still to this day many people are dying because of gun violence and trespassing places killing innocent people and it's only getting worse because parents that own guns and kids fine them , they end up committing suicide.

One event that happened in gun violence history was the mass shooting that happened in Parkland Florida in Marjory Stoneman Douglas high school on February 14th, 2018. During this event Nikolas Cruz, 19 years old entered the high school and shot 17 students including staff members. This event was important because after the shooting young students/ activists came together and formed the "March For Our Lives" campaign to stop gun violence and it became very viral and thousands of people joined to support and to demand a stop. Another example of an event that influenced gun violence is the shooting that happened in Uvalde Texas at Robb elementary school. 18 year old Salvador Ramos entered the elementary school and killed 19 children and a teacher. The cops ended up killing the young man. Questions are still being asked about why the cops took an hour to enter the classroom to rescue the children. Months after the tragedy happened they decided to demolish the elementary school. This change was helpful and impactful because they ended up demolishing the school, no kids or teachers will be attending the school and they don't have to think about what would happen when they enter the school.

In conclusion Gun violence is something we should all care about.its important to care about gun violence because it might not be affecting you but it might be affecting someone close to you, its ending so many peoples lives at a gun age.

Haley Perez

Womens' Rights

From the minute we start walking and talking, the responsibilities women hold are already thrown upon us. In most Hispanic households, you were never the age you really were. Being in an old-fashioned family makes you have to grow up a little faster than other kids your age. Realistically, I was 12, mentally I felt 15 so when I really was 15/16, that's when the whole idea of toxic masculinity, or how we say it, machismo, in Latin cultures really started to hit me, and how I've seen it greatly affect my family especially myself and even my grandma. A few years ago, I was told to start cleaning every Saturday it started off small, I just had to clean the bathroom. It started gradually building up as the years went by. Clean the bathroom, vacuum the sala, clean the salas, clean the kitchen... And so on. Eventually, it was a mutual understanding between my mom and me that it was solely my responsibility to clean the whole house alone. I hated this, I hated having to tackle school 5 times a week and then have to wake up early on a Saturday just to clean instead of taking a break and being a kid. 6 days a week I was busy and had responsibilities on TOP of my own personal difficulties that I was going through at such a young age– from foster care to family screaming matches, the room for stress in my brain was at capacity. I think the worst part of having to grow up in an old-fashioned Hispanic household is all the stereotypes we have to live by. Cook, clean, men don't cry, changing your outfit in my own home just because men are coming over… all things that affect me. Machismo behavior is constantly growing and developing and having a role in this behavior isn't helping me whatsoever. I've seen my grandma overwork herself since I was in kindergarten. Watching her get up to cook for and feed her brother, my uncle, who was a grown man a very much capable of making his own plate of food while I had to pick up after him and clean his dishes while he read El Especialito in the living room. 6 dishes, 2 hands, one sink one person. This is just the state of facts, the facts I have to live and deal with. I've never been one to let these things bother me but I'll never forget this one Saturday during freshman year. I was cleaning the house, as I always do, and I wanted to finish everything quickly to enjoy the rest of my day.. My little brother, who was 8 around the time, was very much capable of picking up a spray and rag to wipe surfaces down–I used this information to my advantage. I asked him for help, expecting compliance due to the simplicity of the task, but instead, this resulted in a screaming match between my little brother and me. My mom heard the fuss and instead of siding with me and just having him help out, she took his side and told me I have no place para mandar a el. I've given up on trying to teach my brother how to clean and do small tasks as such but it's incredibly draining and difficult knowing that every conversation ends with doors slamming and a screaming match between myself and a 9-year-old. Nine years, technically 5 years down the drain as everything we taught him had gone down the drain.

Wouldn't targeting the root of machismo within your own family be simple? You'd think so, but growing up with 3 different generations under one roof only makes this harder. My little brother is being shown that crying is soft and weak y como eres hombre, no puedes llorar(he still does because he is a kid and is human). Toxic masculinity growing up has only made both3 new and old ideologies resurface to the point where my family is constantly struggling to deal with this. To the point where if I'm not good enough at what I'm supposed to do, I get blamed and get called all sorts of things. I think back on my childhood and I convinced myself that it wasn't that bad, that it never once affected me negatively, and that there's no trauma deeply rooted in my childhood, except there is. There is trauma, there are things that affected me negatively, and there were things that essentially caused a butterfly effect in my life. While I can't name any off the top of my head currently, there's still a small part of me that holds a small amount of resentment toward my family for wanting to break the generational curse of machismo in our family. Although it sounds bad, it's true, I do but I don't blame them whatsoever, I never would or could. For they are only going based on their own childhood experiences and don't know how to change anything since its deeply imbedded into our roots.

Devin Pine

The Gun Violence Issue

There are many issues in today's world. A lot of people want social justice. Social justice is fair treatment. So many people are fighting for it since there are many issues that need to be dealt with that have a huge impact on citizens. Such an issue is gun violence. Gun violence is the violent use of guns. This issue has impacted many people by causing them to lose their lives or their loved ones. Those people who have dealt with gun violence end up with PTSD, anxiety and become traumatized. People want to get rid of the use of guns to be more safe. The gun violence issue is important because we need to stop the use of guns so that more people don't lose their lives.

Gun violence is an important issue that we need to care about because many people have lost their lives due to gun violence. Gun violence has been a thing for a long time and has been a huge thing people have discussed. Though it seems to be a huge issue in the present time. There have been many shootings to occur in America. The United

States gun homicide rate is 26 times higher than the other countries (from Everytown for gun safety). America has a lot more shootings than other countries which is why it really needs to be dealt with since many people in America have to deal with deadly shootings. Another thing is that black men are 88 times likely to be shot (from Vital city). So black men have to deal with being shot at a lot which can make black men feel unsafe in their lives. There also have been 306 mass shootings since 2007 which is a huge amount of shootings that occur. That is too many shootings and too many lives being lost and too many people being injured. That is why this issue is a really important issue to be dealt with. To stop mass shootings and avoid people from being killed or injured.

The earliest event that occurred that was related to gun violence was the creation of the NRA (National Rifle Association). This was one of the earliest events to occur and this event was the creation of the NRA and the goal of the NRA was to promote the use of guns. The NRA wanted to promote people to carry around guns or even use them. Though the use of guns can cause many problems so there were some disagreements with the NRA. A law that has been passed that related to gun violence was the second amendment. The second amendment was one of the amendments made out of the 10 amendments to allow people to buy and carry around guns. It gave people the right to bear arms and buy and carry guns with them. Though someone big didin't approve of the violence. Martin Luther King Jr did not believe that violence was the answer to things and wanted peace instead of violence. After his death, people were looking forward to more gun control (Brady united).

An event that has occurred in the present time that has been related to gun violence was the Las Vegas shooting in 2017. Many people have died due to a man that has been shooting people from a window during a concert. 58 people were killed and 800 were injured that day (History.com editors) which brings more attention to why we should deal with gun violence. Though a law that has occurred recently was the Marjory Stoneman Douglas High School Public Safety Act. This law made it so that schools would be more safe. More security and more things in schools to keep students safe. A law that was also passed was the minimum age to purchase a gun. This prohibited people under the age of 21 to get a license to purchase and carry a gun (Giffords law center) so students wouldn't have access to carry a gun and commit a school shooting. Someone that is an advocate for change of gun violence is X Gonzalez. X Gonzalez was a survivor of the Stoneman Douglas High School shooting. From the trauma they experienced, they became an advocate for stricter gun control and wanted no more gun violence to occur (national today).

Gun violence is an important issue that we need to deal with. It is important because Many people lose their lives every day due to gun violence. America has the most mass shootings to occur. If we deal with this issue then less people will lose their lives from the use of guns. I hope that one day, guns will finally be banned. I hope that one day, there will be a law that prohibits people from purchasing and carrying guns with them. Banning the use of guns will be a big step to a better country. People would not lose their lives to guns anymore if we did something about gun violence. There would be less mass shootings and school shootings if we get rid of guns. With less guns, we would not have to worry about going outside, going to school or going anywhere all the time.

Works cited

ACLU Florida, "What Does The 'Marjory Stoneman Douglas High School Public Safety Act' Mean for Students?" ACLU Florida,
https://www.aclufl.org/en/what-does-marjory-stoneman-douglas-high-school-public-safety-act-mean-students

Brady United, "MLK And The Gun Control Act Of 1968" Brady United, 21, January, 2019
https://www.bradyunited.org/blog/mlk-and-the-gun-control-act-of-1968

CNN, "Sandy Hook School Shooting Fast Facts" CNN, 28 November 2022,
https://www.cnn.com/2013/06/07/us/connecticut-shootings-fast-facts/index.html.

Everytown For Gun Safety, "Mass shootings" Everytown For Gun Safety,
https://www.everytown.org/issues/mass-shootings/
.

Giffords Law Center, "Minimum Age to Purchase & Possess In New York," Giffords Law Center, 15 September 2021
https://giffords.org/lawcenter/state-laws/minimum-age-to-purchase-possess-in-new-york/#:~:text=Last%20updated%20September%2015%2C%202021,or%20ammunition%20in%20New%20York.

History.com editors, "Second amendment" A&E Television Networks, 4 December 2017
https://www.history.com/topics/united-states-constitution/2nd-amendment

History.com editors, "Gunman Opens Fire On Las Vegas Concert Crowd, Wounding Hundreds And Killing 58"

A&E Television Networks, 1 October 2018

https://www.history.com/this-day-in-history/2017-las-vegas-shooting

NRA, "A Brief History Of The NRA" NRA,

https://home.nra.org/about-the-nra/

National Today, "Emma Gonzalez" National Today, 11 November 2023

https://nationaltoday.com/birthday/emma-gonzalez/

Vital City, "Data" Vital City,

https://www.vitalcitynyc.org/data_hub?tag=Gun+violence

Kiarelys Ramirez

The Gun Violence Issue

I remember the first time I heard about global warming in my 7th grade Living Environment class. I distinctly recall the vagueness of the explanation: "The earth is going to get a lot warmer!" When I heard my teacher say this, I could only imagine it'd be like summer every day. No worry or anxiety came from hearing this; I was excited because God knows how much I hate the cold. Being uneducated brought me a sense of relief because what I didn't know couldn't harm me, right?

     Wrong. In actuality, my lack of information on climate change was only causing me to be oblivious to the severe climate crisis the world was & is still facing. Nonetheless, it is essential to note that there are two types of ignorance in this world: one being uneducated & the other refusing to be educated. I was not given the proper opportunity to fully grasp the idea of global warming at a young age; however, some people refuse to believe it exists at all. This is a much more dangerous version of ignorance because even when you are fully aware of what is happening, you are choosing to ignore it.

And this is a massive factor in why climate change is not incorporated into the school curriculum as it should be. Teachers only ever touch base with the rising temperatures; they do not explicitly explain the dangers of this crisis climate, for example, frequent natural disasters. But if the government is making less of global warming, it is impossible to expect our teachers to go in-depth about it. Our education depends entirely on avoiding public panic and keeping people uninformed regarding the more severe dilemmas we face. Nonetheless, this is not to say that people aren't working to implement more real-life situations in our schools. In my third year of high school, a new class called Model UN was introduced, and in this class, we were given a chance to look into real issues such as climate change and genocide. I remember being given so much material on global warming that I could call myself a climate change "expert" at 16. I knew so much about it that all I wanted to do was tell everyone, and best believe I did.

Educating as many people as possible about the unspoken climate crisis we are facing needs to be our top priority because we are currently in a race against time. Time is one of the biggest challenges within climate change, along with money, policy & culture. And this is because the situation is only progressing; the effects we are experiencing now are minor, but there'll come a point where they won't be. This is what we need to avoid because once we're passed the tipping point, there is no coming back, and we're destined for complete annihilation.

Now, what are we supposed to do to reverse the effects of climate change & ultimately stop it? To answer this question, we must first understand what this climate crisis is and what is causing it. Climate change, in simplistic terms, is the heating of the earth's temperature due to a significant amount of greenhouse gasses being produced and trapped in the earth's atmosphere. And the production of these greenhouse gasses can be credited to the five grand challenges of climate change: how we make things, how we get around, how we grow things, how we keep cool & warm, and how we plug in.

Everything we do in our daily lives contributes to the number of carbon emissions(greenhouse gasses) we produce, from the AC in your home to the transportation you use to the buildings being built around you. And everything requires some energy, but this isn't necessarily the issue; the problem lies in the type of energy that is being used. In the United States, fossil fuels such as coal, natural gas & petroleum are the primary contributors to greenhouse gas emissions. So that being said, we need to resort to cleaner & more renewable energy sources such as solar and hydropower that will help us get to net zero emissions: producing as close to zero carbon emissions as possible.

Our role in all this may seem insignificant, but it is the jumpstart we need in order to begin addressing this climate crisis. Returning to what I mentioned earlier, education is vital to solving climate change. And now that you have a glimpse of what we are dealing with, you cannot sit around and watch the world burn. It is your responsibility to lend a helping hand to those who are willingly ignorant. The more people are aware of this global matter, the easier we can lobby and the quicker we can reach those who can make a change.

We're Living
In A Man's World

Ever since I was younger, I've always been curvy. A trait that most young girls only possess in the middle to high school. Like every human being on this Earth, I had no control over the makeup of my body, my gender, or my features; it was a present gifted to me by my DNA, my genetic makeup. However, this may be considered the worst present that was given to millions of other women when the gift was followed by being thrown into a world that degrades every being who received this present, the presence of a uterus.

A uterus is a hollow organ present in every woman's body. The organ that has the power to create life out of thin air, the ability to develop hair, nails, toes, and fingers-sounds like a superpower, no? However, as seen throughout history, this superpower often goes unrecognized. Instead, they recognize it as a burden to an obligation. An obligation that forced women to bear children; obligated women to stay home, take care of their husbands, and, god forbid, enter the workplace. No, women must stay home; they must bear children because that's what the uterus is for, right? To bear children - Nothing more, Nothing less.

Men have seen women as incapable of being in the workplace, in power, or in any profession that disregards their initial goal: children, home, and husband. This ideology has crept through centuries, morphing into different forms of misogyny, adapting to the views of the generation present. In the 17th and 18th centuries, women adopted the role of the "perfect wife." Seen in magazines, in the media, and it's become a social norm. Become not became. The idea still lives in the mind of society today, hundreds of years later, in the 21st century. Ideas enforced by those in power, usually white men, influenced how the general public thought and still thinks.

The funny part about misogyny today is that it has adapted to the 21st century so much so that it is unrecognized. Now, even after the progressive and women's rights movements of the past, the great works of women like Susan B. Anthony and Sojourner Truth paved the way for black women to integrate into society somewhat successfully. Though they fought for women as a whole, there was and still is discrimination between black and white women. Not only must I worry about my sex, but also the biases that come from my race as well. It took years for women to integrate into society as human beings with independent decisions, as separate individuals. But we're still unequal. And I say this because the discrimination is a bit more discrete. Women can work now, but are working for less money than men. In the 21st century, women still receive only 83.7% (about .84 of every man's 1.00) of what men gain though they can be working the same job. Another is that a woman can run for president but won't get elected because men won't vote for women. "No. Women are not supposed to be president. Look at our history; do you see a woman president?" It shows that this thought that women are inferior still lurks in a different form. A form that now sees women as sex objects. Once again, objectified, but for another reason now, our appearance.

Men have made up a societal norm of a woman, the "perfect woman." If you fit this description, no matter your age, you automatically qualify to endure sexual comments, sexual behaviors, and overall sexual harassment, whether physical or verbal. This qualification, though not explicitly saying that it forces women to submit to men, forces women to submit to men. Growing up as a girl, this toxic masculinity that I've experienced shows that men don't care about age; there is no age requirement for sexual comments. As I walk down the street, it is normal for a man throws something at me to get my attention. How was he, a grown man, supposed to get my, a 15-year-old child's, attention anyway? As I walk down a dark road alone, a man approaches. As my heart rate doubles and my mind begins to think about all the survival tactics I've learned throughout my years, I ball up my fists, imagining where I will hit first. He walks past, simply thinking about what's for dinner. The fear that possesses me when I see a man instead of a woman at night results from the toxic masculinity that consumes the minds of many men on this planet. I'm safe if he allows it. If he allows it because he doesn't like the answer "no," he'll express anger because I said no to his erotic behavior. The thought that women must say yes, and if not, they'll face the consequences is the ideology that fuels an average male who believes in the gender hierarchy. They want to follow the ways of our "founding fathers ', seven white men who lived almost 200 years ago, when the world was completely different, when society embraced racist, misogynistic views, and when the gender hierarchy prevailed. Well, is the world completely different? Women are at the bottom of the spectrum; in any situation, in any century, women always seem coincidentally to end up below men.

Let's talk about Evolution, the natural process that occurs to organisms over hundreds of years; changes gradually begin to form in order to better the species. Why haven't humans had an ideological evolution? Why haven't we revolutionized our thoughts to realize that women are a part of our species? A very vital role. Animals have shown this, though, through the distinct ways of how females are treated compared to their male counterparts. If you observed a pride of lions, a herd of elephants, or a clan of hyenas, you would notice a trend of female leadership. It's almost as if the female counterpart brings them life, continuing the species. This act alone allows lionesses to eat first, helps the matriarch (oldest, most dominant female elephant) stabilize the herd, and enables willows (female hyenas) to lead when hunting. Homosapians seem not to follow the manuscript for a successful species. They've made the possession of a uterus a chore—an objectification.

Instead of making a phenomenal and almost impossible-to-recreate biological process a tribulation, we can appreciate and cherish the only beings that advance our species: women.

Kiara Rodriguez

The Ending to
Police Brutality

Guns, Weapon, Suites, Bages are all what makes a cop a cop. But what really is a Police officer? Isn't an officer supposed to protect life and property through the enforcement of laws & regulation? So why do we see so many officers abusing their power? What makes them so big and bad? Their job is to keep us safe and many do the exact opposite. There are many social issues impacting the world today but a very important problem people are trying to solve is police brutality. Police brutality is the use of excessive force, usually physical, but potentially in the form of verbal attacks and psychological intimidation, by a police officer. This issue mostly impacts the people who have experienced police brutality firsthand but can also impact families and communities who experience it. Police brutality is very important because police have an obligation to protect the life and rights of a human and to keep their communities safe. So when they abuse their power this is a big issue. Excessive force leads to torture. Torture leads to death. People are and need to help this issue that's going on worldwide and fight for their right to life.

Police brutality is a huge issue and is very important because police have the right to protect our lives not take them. One data point that concerns this issue is, " There are somewhere between 900 and 1,100 people who are shot and killed by police in the United States each year" (NAACP). This shows how so many deaths are caused and lost in the hands of authorities. A huge amount of lives are taken for no reason at all. Another data point that concerns this issue is "A Black person is five times more likely to be stopped without just cause than a white person."(NAACP). This shows how officers racially target black people because of the color of their skin. If this issue is not addressed then racial profiling will continue and progressively get worse.

Police brutality goes all the way down to many years ago. One event that happened in police brutality was Bloody Sunday: Civil rights activists Brutally attacked in Selma. On March 7 1965, in Selma Alabama all the way to the state capitol in Montgomery, police abused and attacked hundreds of people who were at a protest forof civil rights. This protest happened in honor of Jimmie Lee Jackson, a 26 year old activist who was fatally shot in the stomach by police during a peaceful protest. This event was important because all Jimmie wanted was justice and to get a message across the world but instead it resulted in her death by the people who were supposed to protect her life instead. This is only one of the many tragedies that happened throughout history. Many laws have been passed that have helped the lives of many innocent people who were affected by police brutality. A very important law that has been passed is the eighth amendment. The eighth amendment states that no individual shall suffer from cruel or unusual punishment. With that being said this could be interpreted by a court to describe excess and unreasonable force in police brutality (Morgan & Morgan).

While police brutality started many many years ago, It has still gone on til today and have even gotten progressively worse. One recent event that occurred was the death of George Floyed, a 46 year old black man. On May 25, 2020 Floyeds life was taken over a false accusation. An accusation that literally cost him his life. On May 25 the police were called on Floyde by an employee that believed he was trying to buy a pack of cigarettes with a fake $20 bill. Floyde was pinned down by the neck by 3 officers. Floyde being unable to breath showed no signs of life by the time more cop cars showed up. More than one officer had Floyde down. An innocent black man who showed no resistance and listened properly to what he was told (Evan Hill, Ainara Tiefenthaler, Christiaan Triebert, Drew Jordan, Haley Willis, Robin Stein) . Floyed begged for his life. "I can't breathe" came out multiple times from his mouth but no one listened. They saw him as a threat when he wasn't just by the color of his skin. Another recent event that occurred was the death of Breoanna Taylor, a 26 year old woman. Taylor was brutally killed by police on March 13, 2020 a few months before Floyde. Taylor was shot and killed in her apartment during a botched drug raid. Taylors boyfriend who was involved with drugs was the one police were intended to get. He was the reason police were even at Taylors doorstep in the first place. He was then arrested for these drugs. Examinations showed that this raid was very irresponsible and not well planned (Richard A. Oppel Jr., Derrick Bryson Taylor, Nicholas Bogel-Burroughs). These events were and are very important because it shows the lives that were taken in a horrible way. They show the significance of this issue that continues on everyday. Over the years there has been so much word on this issue resulting in people getting involved to create change. One person who is fighting for change within police brutality is Angela Davis. Angela Davis is a political activist who believed racism was a danger to American justice. Angela has formed black lives matter movements and even formed recognisable leadership groups after hearing events that have happened and fought hard for racial injustice (Lanre Bakare).

In conclusion, Police brutality has been a very strong and significant issue that should catch all of our attention and we should all care about. It is important to care about police brutality because we as humans deserve the right to life. Without officers we won't have people to force the law and keep us safe. But with the way some officers abuse their power it doesn't seem like depending on them is a winning situation either. As we move on more into the future we as citizens need to use our voices and platforms more to spread awareness to such a sensitive topic. We need to change the issues in the world. If you want to make the world a better place, look around, and make a change.

Jayden Rolon

Gun Violence

Gun violence is a serious topic that is taking place all over the world. Gun violence refers to the use of firearms to cause harm or death to individuals or groups of people. It is a serious and growing issue in many parts of the world, including the United States. Gun violence takes many forms, including mass shootings, gang violence, and domestic violence. Each year, thousands of lives are lost to gun violence, and countless more are impacted by the physical and emotional trauma it causes.

Mass shootings, in particular, have become all too common in recent years, with high-profile incidents occurring in schools, workplaces, and public spaces. These shootings not only result in loss of life and physical injuries but also leave deep scars on the survivors and the communities affected by them. Gun violence also disproportionately affects marginalized communities, including people of color and low-income individuals, who are more likely to live in neighborhoods with high rates of gun violence.

Addressing gun violence requires a multifaceted approach that involves policy changes, community engagement, and individual responsibility. This may include measures such as stricter background checks for gun purchases, increased funding for mental health services, and targeted interventions to address the root causes of gun violence in high-risk communities. It is essential that we work together to find solutions to this complex issue and ensure the safety and well-being of all individuals, regardless of their background or circumstances.

There have been several incidents of gun violence involving numerous persons, in numerous schools, and elsewhere. On April 20, 1999, a shooting at Columbine High School left several individuals dead, others were hurt, and two people murdered 13 students and one instructor. 21 more individuals were hurt, and three more were hurt while attempting to flee the school. After everything, the two shooters ultimately took their own lives. Although there

Because weapons are so accessible, you can see this occurring all over because people frequently shoot up schools. The problem of school shootings has been around for a while and keeps getting worse. In sixth grade, I recall learning about school shootings and beginning to take shootings seriously. We had lockdowns almost every week in sixth grade, and I remember being somewhat frightened. Located in Littleton, Colorado 80123 at 6201 S Pierce St. High School Columbine. School shootings occur worldwide, but more frequently in the Bronx and New York City than anywhere else. The incident sparked a nationwide discussion about school safety and gun legislation, as well as a significant investigation to ascertain the motives of the teenage gunmen. In the early aftermath of the shootings, it was hypothesized that Klebold and Harris targeted Christians, minorities, and athletes on purpose. One of the gunmen apparently questioned one girl, Cassie Bernall, if she believed in God, according to the initial reports. When Bernall said "Yes," she was fatally shot. Later, in remembrance of their martyred daughter, her parents published a book titled She Said Yes. However, it appears that Bernall was not the one who was asked such a question; rather, another student who had previously suffered gunshot wounds was. The shooter left after that victim said, "Yes," and the shooter. People who commit school shootings either do it because they enjoy it or because they don't like other people.This affected me, and now I take my safety and attending to school seriously. My feelings and perspective have been affected since I can no longer fully trust people because they might be carrying a gun. Due to the current prevalence of school shootings, I am constantly thinking about them.

Gun violence in the world is connected to gun violence in my life because the majority of gun violence that's happening is for no reason, i've had many family members die due to guns for no reason and it hurt me even more when i found that out. Gun violence is a way to show emotion most people who go out and kill tons of people go through things in their life, but there's ways around them from killing people they can always seek a doctor for help or even talk to their family. Gun violence is not only connected to my life, it's connected to everyone's life. At some point someone in their family has died due to a gun of some sort and it's a tragedy. Moreover, gun violence causes significant financial damages. Brady, a group that supports gun regulation, claims that gun violence damages the American economy at least 229 billion dollars annually. Following the shooting at the Robb Elementary School in Uvalde County, Texas, in May 2022, more than 200 CEOs joined together to write a letter pleading with the U.S. Senate to act quickly to reduce gun violence. Gun violence "costs American taxpayers, employers, and communities a staggering 280 billion U.S. dollars per year," according to the letter. There have also been over 15 thousand people who have died due to gun violence this year alone and it's only may, at this rate we might get over 25 thousand people just dying from gun violence which is mindblowing.

Daquan Stevens

Why Is Healthcare So Important?

Inequality and cost are the two causes that widely impact social issues relating to healthcare, and these problems are still going on as of 2023. Although these two causes share significance, plenty of people can't afford healthcare, and the inequity that is involved is continuously making it worse. Healthcare is extremely important and is needed throughout society. When it comes to maintaining health and preventing disease, good healthcare is crucial. If the problems in the healthcare industry are not addressed and are soon to be fixed, then many people may suffer.

Healthcare, also known as the health system, has been used for many decades and is the reason why so many people are as healthy as they are today. One data point that concerts this issue is In 2020, the COVID-19 pandemic put extreme stress on healthcare in the United States alongside other countries ("Health Disparities by Race and Ethnicity.") This means that during the pandemic many were under stress because of the loss of jobs and businesses. Lots of businesses were closed down and people were struggling financially. This impacts the unemployed people due to covid - 19. Hence many people couldn't afford healthcare at the time because of their financial struggle. This was very bad because to fight against COVID-19, people would have to be healthy, but without proper healthcare and the ability to afford people will continue to be unhealthy. More people were likely to get sick because of this and the stressful work of the employers became unbarring for people in the medical field. Another data point that concerns this issue is cost. Throughout the years it has been a high cost of health care. In counting, more than 45% of American adults say that it's difficult to afford health care. Also, more than 40% of people are in medical debt("5 Current Issues in Health Care and What Administrators Can Do".) This means that most of the population in America finds it hard to cover the expenses of healthcare. Also meaning that during the pandemic it was much worse because of the unemployment rate.

One event that happened in this issue's history was the first vaccination. In 1796 Edward Jenner developed the process of vaccination for smallpox. This eventually led to more innovation in vaccinations and many others came up with vaccination to prevent certain diseases. During this event, many people were saved and were prevented from getting smallpox all due to Edward Jenner's innovation that was soon to be used throughout the medical field and still is to this day,. S saving the lives of people around the disease and creating a sense of immunity. In 1980, it was estimated that around 150 to 200 million people were saved due to the creation of smallpox vaccinations. This event is important because, without the use of the vaccinations that are given out now, many people would have died from diseases and viruses because it would be harder to prevent and contain them. Another event that happened in history related to healthcare is thea Ggreat Ddepression. The great depression was a stock market that negatively affected the global economy. Going to a doctor during the Great Depression was difficult because of the fact that money was really hard to come across. Due to this, many people died due to heart disease, and cancer because of the availability of doctors during that time ("The Great Depression changes priorities.") One law that was passed in the past was the consolidated law. It states "membership in any pension or retirement system of the state or of a civil division thereof shall be a contractual relationship, the benefits of which shall not be diminished or impaired." This law is important because all benefits should be implemented for people and I feel like this law is really beneficial for the healthcare industry when it comes to equity. Finally, one person who was fighting to change healthcare was President Richard Nixon. Nixon proposed a limited health insurance reform and wanted the federalization of Medicaid for the poor.

One event that happened recently was the growing provider shortage. The average American needs some help paying for their health expenses, and this is where health insurance comes into play. At the beginning of 2015, many people found it difficult to use their health insurance for specific appointments that had to be paid out of pocket. However, this is a major problem because not everyone can afford the cost of surgeries. During this event, many suffered through diseases, injuries, and other tragedies because of the high cost. In 2021, 64% of uninsured adults said that they were uninsured because the cost of coverage was too high ("Key Facts about the Uninsured Population."). This event is very important because it supports those in bad financial situations and can create a healthy balance in the healthcare system. Also, healthcare is very major and should always be available for all people not depending on their insurance coverage. It not only ensures good physical health but improves the overall well-being of a person. One law that was recently passed that impacts this issue is the health care policy. This law says that "The rules and regulations set forth by lawmakers are implemented in healthcare access, cost, and privacy." It is important because it is good to know that the law is on your side when it comes to understanding how cost can be a big problem for some people across America. Finally, one person who is fighting to change this issue is Michael Dowling. They wanted to improve the struggle while the Covid-19 outbreak was occurring.

In conclusion, healthcare is something we should all care about. It's important to care about healthcare because it helps improve society's well-being as a whole and as a community. In the future, people should take more consideration of healthcare and the importance it has on society today.

Isondra Susana

Climate Change

Climate change refers to long-term climate changes that occur over decades, centuries, or more extended periods. It is produced by rapidly growing greenhouse gasses in the Earth's atmosphere as a result of the use of fossil fuels such as coal, oil, and natural gas. This has been an outgoing issue throughout many centuries and was mainly increased in 1988. You may believe that humans deal with various problems, but we hardly admit that climate change is the most serious of them all, bringing multiple threats.

Climate change has had a negative impact on my entire existence as a result of my knowledge of the weather. Nowadays, the weather has gotten worse, with hot days during spring when temperatures generally range from 60 to 70 degrees Celsius but have reached 80 degrees Celsius in mid-April, clearly due to global warming. This has a negative effect on me since it has caused me to have several colds as my body adjusts to one temperature. However, because it cannot adapt to a single temperature level on a daily basis, it generally decreases in the following days. Climate change also has a negative effect on humans because of the rising intensity and frequency of weather events such as rainstorms. Throughout the years, I have witnessed several high-intensity storms induced by global warming, which have negatively impacted individuals due to the danger of natural disasters to their homes. Hurricane Harvey was one of the most damaging storms caused by temperature changes and influenced by the usage of fossil fuels. Because of how violent and severe this storm was, many people lost their houses and they also lost many family members and many loved ones.

This takes me back to the day my grandmother who lives in Texas had called my mother telling her about how there was a storm forming.
At first, I thought "Oh mami it's probably just a simple little storm."

As the days went by, the storm grew stronger and the categories kept rising to category 4 which was when my family and I had gotten scared. This had a tremendous impact on my grandmother's life because although nothing quite happened to her, the house was impacted tremendously due to all the strong winds. As months passed, they arrived at the fact that this was all due to the impact of f climate change.

There are several methods that can help us to address the climate change challenge. Throughout the last several months of school, I have researched things that we can do to improve society and acknowledge others in regard to climate change. One way we can help combat climate change is to save energy at home because how we heat and cool our homes consumes so much of our electricity. As I gathered information throughout the months, I came to the conclusion that we need to improve our building abilities because if we choose a color that absorbs a lot of sunlight during the summer, we would continue to consume a lot of power.

Another way we can advocatewith climate change is to speak up about how it's affecting us and how we can improve it. According to articles I've read, we could also aim to reduce our use of automobiles since we use a lot of gas and when we run our engines, it messes up the air quality and the air affects us. We can do this by purchasing more electric cars, riding bikes, or going for daily walks.

In conclusion, climate change doesn't just affect me but everyone in general due to the reasoning on how bad the air quality is and how the weather gets intense throughout the years. Although it may be hard to improve climate change, we should make the effort to improve the environment because we are basically losing more than gaining due to all the circumstances depicted in this research.

Christian Torres

The Implications of Gun Violence

There are many social justice issues impacting the world today. One problem people are trying to address is gun violence because it is one of the biggest challenges we face currently. People are fighting against gun violence because it has taken many lives and peoples loved ones. Gun violence is nothing new and has been happening for a long period of time. Gun violence activists and people of different communities are trying to stand up against the use of guns so that nobody else will get hurt. I chose this social justice issue because it is also something happening in our community as well. This social justice issue is important because it keeps continuing and gets worse. Gun violence is something that needs to be talked about more and taken more seriously.

It's important to care about gun violence because it's something that can happen to you and it has impacted others lives. One data point that concerns this issue is more than 11,500 people in the U.S. have been killed by gun violence in 2023 only. This means that hundreds of people are dying everyday to gun violence whether it be suicide, murders, or mass shootings. This can impact innocent bystanders because of how easy it can be to access guns and let it get into the wrong person's hands. Another data point that concerns this issue is the number of deaths per year due to gun violence in New York. On average, over 800 people die from gun violence every year and over 2000 get wounded. This means that gun violence rates are high and are getting out of control, even in our own community. If this issue is not addressed, then it means gun violence rates will only continue to increase and spiral out of control in the U.S.

One event that happened involving gun violence is Abraham Lincoln's Death. It happened on April 4th, 1865. During this event, Abraham was attending a show in Ford's Theatre when John Wilkes Booth had assassinated him. This event was important because he was the president of the United States, and he had ended slavery for African Americans. Another event that happened in history was the Kent State University Shooting. This event took place on May 4, 1970. During this event, members of the Ohio Nnational Gguard started shooting at a crowd of Kent State University students, killing 4 and injuring 9 people. This event was important because it had a direct impact on national politics. One law that was passed in the past was the gun control act of 1964. This law imposed federal licensing of individuals to manufacture or deal in firearms and banned all interstate transportation of weapons to people who were not licensed as importers, collectors, manufacturers, or dealers. One person that was fighting to change this issue was President Lyndon B. Johnson. He wanted to make sure that gun laws were more strict and make sure that it didn't get into the hands of the wrong people, therefore he made the gun law.

One event that happened involving gun violence is the Parkland High School Shooting. This tragedy happened on February 14, 2018. During this event, a gunman entered the highschool and started shooting at staff and students. 17 people were killed that day and another 17 were injured. This event was important because it was one of the biggest mass shootings in U.S. history. Another event that happened recently was the Las Vegas Strip Massacre. This event took place on October 1st, 2017. During this event, a gunman had opened fire at a music festival in Las Vegas, killing 58 people that night and injuring hundreds of others. This event is important because it is the deadliest mass shooting in U.S. history. One law that was recently passed that impacts gun violence was the assault weapons ban of 2023. This law bans the sale, import, and manufacture of military style assault weapons and high capacity magazines. It is important because many shootings have happened when people got access to these types of weapons. Congress is fighting for this change and banned the transfer and possession of machine guns.

In conclusion, gun violence is something we should all care about. It's important to care about gun violence because it is changing the world and taking innocent people's lives. In the future, I hope that the U.S. will make stricter gun laws and limit who can have access to guns. Gun violence rates have been increasing over the last few years and hopefully we will be able to put a stop to it.

Death Is Coming
Faster Then Ever

Drought, storms, heat waves, rising sea levels, melting glaciers and warming ocean. This can directly harm animals and human kind. This also destroys the places we live in. Earth. This is only half of the things that global warming and climate change have done to us. Even though there are other social issues around the world or in the U.S, I think that the most important one is environmental change. Changes in the environment are caused by both natural and human processes. Energy and materials are transformed and transported by environmental systems and human activities, contributing to environmental changes. This includes problems like overpopulation, pollution, burning fossil fuels, and deforestation.

Us talking about this problem is very important to us. Many people don't care that we need to help or do better in the world. They say that it doesn't affect them, but what they don't see is that it's affecting them and the world. Global warming is one of the environmental impacts that have on us. Research from the UN, says "Global warming can result in many serious alterations to the environment, eventually impacting human health. It can also cause a rise in sea level, leading to the loss of coastal land, a change in precipitation patterns, increased risks of droughts and floods, and threats to biodiversity" (Mohamed). This tells us that not only does it hurt the environment but that it also hurts human health. It also says about the coastal land, global warming has caused glaciers to melt in the arctic which means if it mealthing then the sea level will rise. This creates floods in places next to the coast.

Throughout the years, most of the governments try to help the world. They try to make the world a better place, but most of the time the things are bad or good. For example, back in the 1970s . when a senator from Wisconsin organized a national demonstration and made a special day called Earth Day. The first Earth Day was celebrated in 1970, when a United States senator organized a national demonstration to raise awareness about environmental issues. A big person that has been fighting for this change is Al Gore. In the past few decades, Gore has been actively involved in environmental work. Gore hosted the first congressional hearings on global warming and toxic waste when he was 28 years old, after joining the House of Representatives. Al Gore once said in one of his interviews " We're still putting 162 million tons [of greenhouse gas] into it every single day and the accumulated amount is now trapping as much extra heat as would be released by 600,000 Hiroshima-class atomic bombs exploding every single day on the earth," Gore said. He says that everyday we keep trapping the gasses in our atmosphere which trap heat and is the reason that we have been having so many heat strikes or other things that happen because of heat. For example the heat causes the ice in Antarctica to melt which causes the sea level to rise.

Some current laws that have been happening recently was the government doing something called zero emissions or net zero. What this means is that it's been a target to completely negate the amount of greenhouse gasses produced by human activity. And to be achieved by reducing emissions and implementing methods of absorbing carbon dioxide from the atmosphere. However, reaching Net Zero alone isn't sufficient. Since some climate change is not always lasting, even if the world were to stop all carbon emissions tonight the effects of the emissions that have already occurred will still remain for decades. So most things the government can help to try to help with the world it isn't going to always help or be effective to us.

In conclusion, environmental impact is something we should all care about. This issue is very important because we live on this planet and if something bad were to happen then we will all die. But in the future in the 2050s most governments believe that it will probably be good if we all follow the zero emission laws. Many people don't think that this is dangerous. But global warming or any other things are bad. For example global warming causes climate change, which poses a serious threat to life on Earth in the forms of widespread flooding and extreme weather. This or any other issue that is caused by environmental impact which can cause many damage to our planet.

Melvin Vasquez

Women's Rights

One problem that people are trying to address is women rights. Women rights is a protest of a movement about women fighting for their own freedom and want to be equal and not be treated like garbage and forgotten like it, noting what they want is to be free and have their own opinion and right to be a citizen.

People are fighting to help women to have a great relationship and it is not only about the women in the United state in general all women around the world that still struggle to have let say like female immigrants. who struggle to have freedom and equality to other people like men who have freedom and right to speak out so as womens.

Women rights are important and the reason why is that all women are supposed to be equal and treated the same amount just like mens and this could show that many womens have to deal these harsh life experience dealing with sexual violence and the banned of abortion in most some part of the untied state due to the supreme court choses to bannad this process for all women how does not want prenancy and does not wanted a child and now the supreme court in different state banning it and as humans women are not to be treated like a object but like a real people to be treated fairly.

It important to care about this women right because lot of women are now struggle to have peace of their own and this could tell that women and of course immigrant as well were struggle to have the same equal pay of money just like men do in their own jobs plus their a lot of women who still struggle of relationship of mens because this a lot of men around the united state of report of sexual violence and other crimes that were based of womens were dating in a wrong certain age and had experience of violence and abused for those type of men.

According to the research 1 of my social issue that the metoo movement is about a movement to support younger women who have been experience of sexual violence and having relationship of mens in a different age that are not in the same age what young women are plus to support younger women to stop sexual violance and against sexual violane and top protest od stoping sexual violance around the globe.

This means that the sexual violence and dathing people in different age is a crime and it should not be allowed that to women and should not be allowed women to deal with these abused and this impact a lot of people and even young girl to know that this issue it still happening to this day women are still fight ing to have their own right and freedom and never wanted to be lay on in sexual violance again.

If the issue is not addressed then those people should be accountable.

One event that happened in this issue's history was the Seneca Falls convention during the 1800 womens were not able to be free or do like they weren't able to vote and weren't able to have a abortion. It happened in New York City at the Wesleyan Chapel in the 1800s. During this event the Seneca Falls march was about a protest for women to have their own right to be free of abortions and vote. This event was important because if mens were able to vote the women should be equal to vote. The abortion law is important because women should have a choice to do whatever they want with their body. Another event that happened in history was Roe v Wade because this event was for womens to have abortions legal in every state. Women everywhere should have their choice to do with their own body.

It happened in Dallas,Texas in 1973. During this event Roe v Wade the supreme court recognized that the right of liberty and the landmark US court have the right of an abortion. This event was important because all women should have their own choice of doing whatever they want to do with their body and they are not be forced to have pregnancy and have the right to have an abortion. One law that was passed in the past was the 19 amendment because this law was about the fight for women 's freedom and having their right to vote and fighting against the laws during the 1920. This law said that now women rights of citizens of the united state are now to vote shall not abiding in the united state or in any other state.

It is important because women's choices are allowed to speak up and they could do whatever they want if they wanted to vote and have their right to equal meaning because if men are able to vote then the women are able to vote.

Finally, one person who was fighting to change within this issue was beginning in the 1800's. Women are organized, petitioned, and picketed to win the right to vote, but it took them decades to accomplish their purpose.

They wanted to have a freedom speech of why womens should be able to vote and to vote for whoever they wanted and have civil disobedience to the strict laws and they want to change the law that granted women free to vote.

One event that happened recently was the repeal of Roe v. Wade because this event was about the supreme court overturned the Roe v Wade abortion right and banned abortion in most of the states.
It happened in June 2022 in mississippi.

During this event people are protesting because the supreme court has overturned the Roe v Wade law of the 1973 decision that established a constitutional right and now the supreme court wants to overturn the law for having a abortion in the united states.

This event is important because the supreme count want to banned some states of having the right to have an abortion and women of this current area are not to treated like unequal and having their own choice of their body and now they may no longer have the same freedom of having abortion and the states are having their decision of whether or not the right of abortion could legal or illegal.

One law that was recently passed that impact this issue is the original Roe v Wade abortion right. This impacted this issue because this was the start of women having an abortion in the United state.

The law says that the decision whether to continue or end a pregnancy belongs to the individual, not the government.

It is important because these laws could make a change to women because they do not want pregnancy or have a child and all abortion in the united state and if abortion are illegal the united state could be overpopulated.

Finally,one person who is fighting to change within this issue was the protector, and the womens.

They wanted womens to have choices for themself to have abortion do not want to have a child and the Constitution of the United States generally protects a pregnant individual's liberty to have an abortion.

In conclusion women right is something we should all care about because they are human that should be treated like citizen and have their choice to do whatever they want in their life and they should not be left aside and have equally like mens are and it the mens are able to vote so as women could vote of how they want and likes because if we didn,t then women will still struggle to this day.

It's important to care about (women's rights) because they are people who wanted freedom and peace and they wanted to be in families of equality of vote,jobs and abortion as plus women are not meant to be controlled but they are meant to have their own freedom and liberty and justice in this world.

In the future I hope that women can live peacefully and have equality in this world. Women have the right to protest and fight for their right against any strict laws that do not show them respect and are treated like citizens but i wish that in the future women will be able to have freedom.

Author Bios

Class Photos

Ms. Bloodworth—4th Period Class

Ms. Bloodworth—7th Period Class

Ms. Bloodworth—8th Period Class

MIRANDA AMILL

Miranda Amill is a student at Morris Academy for Collaborative Studies. She was born in the Bronx, New York where she currently lives. Last year, she got an award for being in the Honors Society and was acknowledged by the whole school. She loves listening to rap and drill music, traveling with her family, going to see her boyfriend, and participating in her religious events. She hopes to be the best doctor in the world.

CRYSTALYN BOAHENE

Crystalyn Boahene is a student at Morris Academy for Collaborative Studies. She is in the 11th grade. She is an American who was born and currently lives in the Bronx. She has made the Principal's List and has won an award in language class. She loves listening to music, watching movies, and participating in sporting activities like soccer, basketball, softball, and many others. Her favorite movie is "War Room." She hopes to one day have a Bachelor's in Business Management and also help in the development of the societies.

HECTOR BUENO

Hector Bueno is a student at Morris Academy for Collaborative Studies. He was born in the Dominican Republic and currently lives in New York. He always tries his hardest to do all the work he needs to do. He loves watching anime and reading manga. He hopes to graduate high school and major in computer science. He also wants to learn Japanese so that he could travel to Japan.

GIANCARLOS CARRILLO

Giancarlos Carrillo is an 11th grade student at Morris Academy for Collaborative Studies. Giancarlos Carrillo was born in the Bronx, New York. In 8th grade, Giancarlos won an award for participation. Giancarlos loves to listen to music and likes to travel during free time. Giancarlos hopes one day to work in public transportation.

JHONNY CASTELLON

Jhonny Castellon is a student at Morris Academy for Collaborative Studies. When he was 13, he beat 100% of master mode in "The Legend of Zelda: Breath of the Wild." He loves listening to many different types of music, watching anime, and reading manga. After high school, he hopes to find a good job that pays well to help his family.

CHINWENDU CHIBUZO

Chinwendu Chibuzo is a student at Morris Academy for Collaborative Studies. He was born in Lagos, Nigeria and currently lives in the Bronx, New York. In 8th grade, he made the boys basketball team for the first time. He loves playing basketball, listening to music, and eating rice and chicken. He hopes to become an entrepreneur to help out people with his business.

JHON DE LA CRUZ

Jhon De La Cruz is a student at Morris Academy for Collaborative Studies. He attends a robotics club in school. He is very good at math and is in the 11th grade. He was born In Caguas, Puerto Rico and now living in the Bronx, NY. In the 10th grade, he discovered what he wanted to do as a career. He loves working with technology of every kind. He hopes one day to be a great engineer and buy his mom her dream shop.

DANIEL NOCEDA

Daniel Noceda is currently a student in Morris Academy For Collaborative Studies. He was born In the Bronx and grew up in Harlem till he was 9. He grew up knowing his life was different from others as he was a child of undocumented immigrants, but he knew that was no excuse and always trys his best. He is currently part of the schools SLT team, Student Ambassador, Future MET intern and is running for School President. After graduation he hopes to make his family proud by joining the Air-force and pave the road for the rest like him.

COBY GALARZA

Coby Galarza is a student at Morris Academy for Collaborative Studies. He has many classes such as APUSH, AP Computer Science, Geometry, and Health. He was born in the Bronx, New York and comes from a Latino background with Mexican parents. In 11th grade, he won a bronze trophy in a tournament for squash tournament for Squash and continues to rise in his ranking. He loves to play many sports, listens to music, and loves to experience new things. After graduating high school, he hopes to go to a good college to pursue a Bachelor's degree in any major. After college, he plans to have a good paying job that makes him enjoy work.

NOELIA GALINDO

Noelia Galindo is a student at MACS. She is a junior looking forward to graduating next year. She was born in Manhattan and was raised in the Bronx. In elementary school, she won awards for coming to school everyday. She likes to listen to music and would like to travel one day. She hopes to one day become a doctor or a veterinarian.

NICOLE GILLYARD

Nicole is a student at Morris Academy for Collaborative Studies. Nicole was born in Harlem, NY but currently resides in Bronx, NY. She been on A/B and A honor roll for each grade she has completed and various athlete awards. Nicole participates in varsity softball, soccer and volleyball, and manages the boys and girls basketball teams. She loves listening to R&B and soul music whenever she can, and plays multiple sports, but her favorite is softball. Her favorite movie is Me Before You, and her favorite book is When You Were Everything.

CRISTAL GONZALEZ

Cristal Gonzalez is a student at Morris Academy for Collaborative Studies. She was born in Harlem, New York and currently lives in the Bronx, New York. In 7th grade, she won an award for showing a lot of progress in math. She loves listening to music, eating, trying new things, and dancing. She hopes that one day she becomes a cosmetologist and an ultrasound tech.

RASHIDA ISSAKA

Rashida Issaka a student of Morris Academy Collaborative Studies. She was born in Ghana and now lives in the Bronx, New York. In 3rd grade, she was an athletic girl and won some awards for taken part in the activities. She likes to listen to different music and eat local food from her country, like banku with okra stew and jollof. She hopes to become a good nurse who takes care of people in the world.

ISABEL LANCE

Isabel Lance is a junior at Morris Academy for Collaborative Studies. She was born and raised in the Bronx, NY. After school she spends her time volunteering in her community and working at a cafe. She loves to paint, read, watch crime shows like "Criminal Minds" and hopes to make a difference in the world especially in the justice system. Isabel chose to write about LGBTQ+ discrimination because being a member of the community she has a unique experience that many may have not and thought it was fitting to share. After she is done with high school, she hopes to attend CSU: Dominguez Hills to study political science. She plans to go to law school and receive her Juris Doctor to become a criminal justice defense attorney.

MELANIE MELLA

Melanie Mella is a student at Morris Academy for Collaborative Studies. In school, she is a PGC leader and hopes to be the next Head of Publicity for Student Government next year as a senior. She is an immigrant from the Dominican Republic and has lived in the Bronx, New York since she was 7 years old. She enjoys listening to different types of music especially artists like Kali Uchis or Ariana Grande, etc., and watching The Vampire Diaries. After high school, she plans to go to John Jay College of Criminal Justice to major in criminology in hopes of becoming an FBI Agent.

ANDRIW NUÑEZ

Andriw Nuñez is an 11th grade student at Morris Academy for Collaborative Studies. He is part of the National Honor Society as well as a Student Ambassador for his school helping teachers when it's needed. He was born in Manhattan, New York, moving around in that area a lot before moving and residing in the south Bronx.

KILIAN OGOWAN

Kilian Ogowan is a student at Morris Academy for Collaborative Studies. He was born in France and currently lives in the Bronx, New York. In 8th grade, he won "Student of the Month" three times, which was considered his academic 3-peat. He loves playing basketball and video games along with watching shows and movies. He loves his clothing as well and shops often. He hopes to one day make it in the world by making lots of money and living comfortably like he always wished to when he is older with a good paying job that he actually enjoys doing while helping and benefiting others.

DAINA PEREZ

Daina is a student at Morris Academy for Collaborative Studies. She was born in Santo Domingo, Dominican Republic, and currently lives in the Bronx, New York. In elementary school, she won Student of the Month all 6 years and also won a prize for Most Intelligent. She loves listening to Brent Faiyaz and Drake, traveling, and watching a lot of shows. She hopes to one day become really successful and rich in life, and to follow her dreams all the time.

DEVIN PINE

Devin is a 11th grade student at Morris Academy for Collaborative Studies. He was born in the Bronx, New York and still lives in the Bronx. In 10th grade and in middle school, he made honor roll for his grades in his classes. He loves to listen to music, play video games, and play football. He hopes to become good at making music and live his dream of becoming a music producer and be known for his music.

KIARELYS RAMIREZ

Kiarelys Ramirez is a junior in high school at Morris Academy for Collaborative Studies. She was born in Bayamon, Puerto Rico, and currently lives in New York. She Is a student ambassador in her school, working and helping the staff with whatever they need. She is interested in Criminal Justice and hopes to go to the College of John Jay to later become a police officer when she graduates.

JAYDEN ROLON

Jayden Rolon is a student at Morris Academy for Collaborative Studies. He is a student in the 11th grade. He was born and raised in The Bronx, New York. He's made honors rolls multiple time throughout my high school experience so far. He loves listening to Drake, visit new places, and helping my family. His favorite show so far is "Outer Banks". He hopes to become a veterinarian one day in my life time.

ISONDRA SUSANA

Isondra Susana, a student at Macs, enjoys reading poetry and science. She was born in the Dominican Republic and moved to New York when she was four years old. She was a quick learner who excelled in elementary and middle school. Despite many challenges, she would always strive for success; she is aiming for an advanced diploma and a 3.0 GPA when she graduates from high school. As the years flied by she has discovered her true passion in majoring in the medical field.

JOEL TORRES

Joel Torres is a student at Morris Academy for Collaborative Studies. He was born in the Bronx, New York, where he lives today. In 8th grade, he went through a rough time because of COVID, but it didn't stop him from graduating. He loves to listen to Peso Pluma and Bad Bunny, play video games, and sleep when he can. He hopes to one day become the best cop so that people can view them differently.

www.ingramcontent.com/pod-product-compliance
Lightning Source LLC
Chambersburg PA
CBHW080413290526
45791CB00008BA/2262